A Nation of Family and Friends?

T0384369

Critical Issues in Sport and Society

Michael A. Messner, Douglas Hartmann, and
Jeffrey Montez de Oca, Series Editors

Critical Issues in Sport and Society features scholarly books that help expand our understanding of the new and myriad ways in which sport is intertwined with social life in the contemporary world. Using the tools of various scholarly disciplines, including sociology, anthropology, history, media studies, and others, books in this series investigate the growing impact of sport and sports-related activities on various aspects of social life as well as key developments and changes in the sporting world and emerging sporting practices. Series authors produce groundbreaking research that brings empirical and applied work together with cultural critique and historical perspectives written in an engaging, accessible format.

For a list of all the titles in the series, please see the last page of the book.

A Nation of Family and Friends?

Sport and the Leisure Cultures of British Asian Girls and Women

AARTI RATNA

Rutgers University Press

New Brunswick, Camden, and Newark, New Jersey

London and Oxford

Rutgers University Press is a department of Rutgers, The State University
of New Jersey, one of the leading public research universities in the nation.
By publishing worldwide, it furthers the University's mission of dedication
to excellence in teaching, scholarship, research, and clinical care.

Library of Congress Cataloging-in-Publication Data

Names: Ratna, Aarti, author.
Title: A nation of family and friends? : sport and the leisure cultures of
British Asian girls and women / Aarti Ratna.
Description: New Brunswick, NJ : Rutgers University Press, [2024] | Series: Critical
issues in sport and society | Includes bibliographical references and index.
Identifiers: LCCN 2023027104 | ISBN 9781978834125 (hardcover) |
ISBN 9781978834118 (paperback) | ISBN 9781978834132 (epub) |
ISBN 9781978834156 (pdf)
Subjects: LCSH: South Asians—Great Britain—Social conditions | South
Asians—Great Britain—Social life and customs. | Women—Great Britain—Social
conditions. | Sports for women—Social aspects—Great Britain. | Sports for
girls—Social aspects—Great Britain. | BISAC: SPORTS & RECREATION /
Cultural & Social Aspects | SOCIAL SCIENCE / Race & Ethnic Relations
Classification: LCC DA125.S57 R38 2024 | DDC 305.48/8914041—dc23/eng/20231208
LC record available at https://lccn.loc.gov/2023027104

A British Cataloging-in-Publication record for this
book is available from the British Library.

References to internet websites (URLs) were accurate at the time of writing.
Neither the author nor Rutgers University Press is responsible for URLs
that may have expired or changed since the manuscript was prepared.

∞ The paper used in this publication meets the requirements of the
American National Standard for Information Sciences—Permanence
of Paper for Printed Library Materials, ANSI Z39.48-1992.

rutgersuniversitypress.org

For Lennie and Saffron

Contents

Preface

Sibling Rivalries

My sister and I are proxy guardians of young people. She teaches at a secondary school, and I teach in the higher education sector. We regularly have conversations about inequalities in the workplace. When I discuss issues of racism, sexual abuse, or unfair workplace practices, her advice is usually the same: "Ignore it" and, most recently, "If the student doesn't complain, why do you care?" My commitment to feminism as a political and personal choice profoundly shapes everything that I see, and once seen—for me and others (e.g., Ahmed 2017)—it cannot be unseen or forgotten. I feel the need to intervene even if I do not know how.

At the start of my academic career, for instance, I taught at a local further education (FE) provider where most of the students were from socially deprived communities. They were mostly African and Caribbean or South Asian, and many of their lived realities demonstrated to me—even if not to my sister, who also worked at the same institution—that they had been let down by the education system. While I loved teaching these young people, I could not reproduce the "lie" (Giroux 2000, 2003; Mirza 2008) of education as a democratic environment that would support their upward socioeconomic mobility. From my time teaching sport studies at this FE college, the only student whose prospects I know about now is an African Caribbean man who left partway through his studies. I was pleased to find out that he did not become the drug dealer he professed he aspired to be, but perhaps more unsurprisingly, representative of many in his local community, he is working in a manual labor job (see also Campbell 2020). I will never forget my first day teaching at this college. It was the first time I witnessed a boy (sixteen years old) "fake hump" one of the girls (also sixteen years old) during a practical session playing football (known as soccer in other parts of the world). Apparently, it was "a joke." The girl in question felt violated. The joke was not funny. She complained to a member of staff who was responsible for student behavior management. An apology followed, but the boy in question faced no other serious consequences; he was neither suspended nor excluded from the college.

Thinking back to this time, I am frustrated that I must spell out to my sister that many young women (and men) are violated by people they know and that they can be groomed by trusted adults, including teachers, sports coaches, and those in positions of institutional authority (Ahmed 2021; Brackenridge 2001; Hartill 2009; Owton 2016). This sexual violence is racialized and classed too (Ferguson 2003; Lorde [1984] 2007; Lowe 2015; Manalansan 2003; Muñoz 2009; Puar 2007). How would my sister feel if she knew that I had experienced such confusing forms of control at the secondary school that we both attended? A place where she experienced bullying and I, on the other hand, as the popular sporty sister (see interlude 1), received unwanted attention from a dual-heritage male teacher. I had initially read this teacher to be a White Englishman; I found out otherwise when one day he announced, "Your skin color is the same as my mother's." Many of my British Asian friends had similar brown skin, so what was so "special" about mine that he had to pass a comment? I was surrounded by a large group of wonderful friends who felt like family, bonded as we were after playing various sports together at school. At the time, though, I do not think these friends would have believed me even if I had disclosed this comment to them—or other advances that had occurred. I was a teenager with little life experience, and he was a grown man, in his twenties, popularly considered by students as one of the attractive teachers. I still feel "weird" (I cannot find a better word). Did I imagine it? Although I have discussed sexual harassment with my sister in more recent times to continue to seek corroboration that this male teacher behaved inappropriately, my sister is still unable to make the link between my school-based experience and my desire to challenge injustices in sport, education, and society now. I know my sister would not want me to be or feel hurt. Nonetheless, I have always experienced our sibling relationship as in tension—on the edge of exploding and/or inclusive of sporadic moments of closeness and rapport. Many thoughts and feelings about our sisterhood remain unspoken, filling the affective void between us.

Practicing Self-Care

While discussions with my sister are arguably a personal matter, they represent the lived ambiguities of people's family relationships (Anzaldúa 1987; Lugones 2003; Tillmann 2015). In this book, I explore how we make social attachments to others, whether as "blood" (familial relations) or "blud" (friends who do not share familial bloodlines; see the introduction for further debate). Both family and friend relationships can take plural and complex forms (Chowdhury and Phillipose 2016). Like other social relations, they are dynamic sites: they can be joyful, sincere, pleasurable, and also deeply painful. While scholars of sport and leisure have for some time explored the impact of family and peer group social relations upon involvement in sport (see, e.g., Coakley 2011; Laker 2012; Trussell and Jeanes 2021), this is not my focus. Like Carter (2007) and Webster (2022), who write about the politics of migration (albeit in different contexts), I am concerned with how family and friends, as organizing concepts, support ways of knowing the social world (and my place in it).

It is not always a conscious and/or intentional practice, but for me, writing down the things I have experienced, seen, and heard in my relationships with my family and friends also provides an opportunity to make introspective reflections about power (as it relates to race, ethnicity, gender, sexualities, class, dis/ability, age, and the nation). This writing also represents a form of embodied knowledge formation—my erotic (Lorde [1984] 2007). It is a re/presentation of "my" life that speaks back to powerful discourses about "who we are" from our shared racialized, nondisabled, gendered, sexual, and changing class, age, and generational standpoints. As a fortysomething woman currently living in the north of England, I write about family and friends "as I see it" not to start bloody warfare, even though such conflicts do arise within family and friendship relationships, but to recognize that the acts of thinking and writing are also acts of self-care—knowing my family and friends as a defining act of knowing (and accepting) myself in a world where life chances unfairly separate communities of people and differentially impact our respective life chances and psychic well-being (see also Anzaldúa 1987; Lugones 2003; McGuire-Adams 2020a, 2020b; McGuire-Adams et al. 2022). Healing from systems of discrimination and abuse does not just take time (i.e., feeling better or happier as time progresses); it requires learning how to survive interlocking institutions (e.g., of education and sport) that are designed to be exclusive rather than inclusive. The "rules" that govern these spaces continue to be unfathomable to me (Puwar 2004). Occupying "the house" (sporting or educational) that was built to serve the White male colonial "master" (see Lorde [1984] 2007), until dismantled and remade anew, can only ever be harmful to men and women of color (e.g., Emejulu 2022; see also McGuire-Adams 2021).

I gave myself time to start writing this book even before I had secured a publication contract. It was important for me to think through my thoughts before I sent them out into the world for public and academic scrutiny. Often, thoughts about the institutional context of sport and education (and how it overlaps) were dark and painful (see also Ratna 2017a), yet, nevertheless, I enjoyed being "in" my head—to feel soothed and to garner pleasure from thinking and writing. It was also time (not always quiet with children in the background) to be "true" to my own "inside" voice (as much as I consciously could be) and to quiet the voices of peers, friends, and colleagues, some of whom (to me, at least) are tantamount to being academic "arseholes" (Littler and Emejulu 2019)—that is, those who write about sport and social justice, for instance, but fail to take responsibility for their own complicities in reproducing structures of inequity and control (see also McGuire-Adams 2021). In my frustration with such people, even those who have been friends, I wrote in sporadic and unstructured ways: streams of consciousness. Other times, I did not write at all—when writing as a form of self-care concomitantly reminded me of the intense anxiety caused by having to work and be "in" the elite, White, nondisabled, and gendered sites of higher education. Then, occasionally, I would fall into deeply focused periods of writing when arguments "in my head" coherently came "to life." This kind of private writing, for me, is a self-indulgent and privileged act that brought me back to family, friends, and those significant others who were/are part of my life story so far. From this process, I increasingly began to utilize the concepts of family and friends to provide an analytical tool, to explore the stories of other South Asian women whose experiences of sport and/or education were similar to as well as different from my own. I write this book for "us"/them.

Of Blood and Blud

The social categorization of humans as racial and ethnic groups of people continues to be plagued by positivistic assumptions about how the social world is ordered. Arguably, there is an overriding tendency to draw on biological sciences to demarcate different flora and fauna—specifically, that is, the social categorizations used to mark and distinguish "family" groups of animal and plant life. In contemporary times, the scientific legacies of such thinking are no more present than in neofascist discourses that continue to promulgate "race" as a scientific "truth" (Thangaraj et al. 2018). Supposedly, this is a truth that people are "too scared" to talk about (Entine 2000). From such a populist viewpoint, the greatest damage to harmonious and peaceful human relations is alleged to spring from the minds of those obsessed with political correctness; they supposedly "see" racism when it is not even there (for further debate, see Thangaraj et al. 2018). Not only is this argument a grotesque fantasy that further masks the bloody, violent, and real experiences of living in a racist and discriminatory world, but it serves to hide "White" as a racial category (King 2008, 2009; McDonald 2009; Watson and Scraton 2001, 2017).

Many scientists have long accepted that "race" is a false category, masking genetical variations within assumed "racial" groups as well as overlaps across "racial" groups. Historically, the notions of family and blood have had deadly (and symbolically violent) consequences (e.g., slavery, the Holocaust, genocide). Yet race continues to be popularly used as a discursive category to demarcate different groups of people, often signified through phenotypical features such as skin color. However, *blood* or *blud* as colloquial terms of endearment, between those who recognize themselves as kith and kin, is about more than racial science. *Blud* is an idiom that travels across time and space, including spaces of sport and leisure, as an expression of resistance to racism and, sometimes, as an affectionate greeting between friends (across racial differences). Arguably, *family* and *friends*, as "blood" or "blud," are meaningful terms that can be used to make sense of racialized forms of being and belonging.

Blood for South Asian communities, as for many Black communities (Collins 2000), is often tied to problematic colonial tropes (see, e.g., Carrington 2010; St. Louis 2003; Spracklen 2008), reproducing false binaries about "White" people as superior to "South Asian" people (see chapter 1). Interestingly, in India, for instance, the social construction of race has power because it is linked to quasi-religious sentiments about the "purity" of blood. Based on a Hindu belief system concerning class and occupational destiny (Virali and Rao 2019), it is purported that people are hierarchically organized, with Brahmins higher up the social order as an elite caste (closest to godliness) and Dalits, who are positioned as the lowest caste, as "untouchables" (unhuman). In India, categorizations of caste are social proclivities that do not necessarily demand the avoidance of racial contamination (i.e., through interracial marriages) but rather propel the impulse to avoid—at all costs—diluting elite class and caste cultural distinctions (i.e., through intercaste marriages). Virali and Rao (2019, 53) further suggest that the legacies of casteism in India are so rigid that one solution to challenging its structuring power would be "through the fusion of blood" so that the feeling of being kindred rather than alien would vanish. The significance of race, class, and caste are further developed in relation to gender and debates about the nation in interlude 1 and chapter 3. Suffice it to suggest, for now, that patriarchy and heterosexuality are often reproduced through such racial, classist, and caste systems of living in and across the Indian diaspora (see Paik 2019 for further detail). Aware of the linguistic and scientific repertories of "race" that reproduce complex hierarchies of race, gender, class, and caste, it is my intention in this book to use *family* and *friends* with care. More specifically, I wish to unpick the dynamics of race, gender, and nation to produce an empirical and cultural analysis of the sporting and leisure lives of British Asian girls and women.

A Definitional Note

For definitional purposes, I refer to women of the South Asian diaspora as those whose familial heritages stem from the Indian subcontinent, including the countries of Afghanistan, Bangladesh, India, Myanmar, Nepal, Pakistan, and Sri Lanka. However, in writing across diaspora space, it is not my intention to "fix" colonial and neocolonial hierarchies, recognizing that places of "home" (within South Asia) and "away" (across the spaces and places where South Asian people have traveled to and across) represent shifting, complex, and imperial geographies (Ali, Kalra, and Sayyid 2006; Brah 1996; Simpson 2016; Tuck and Yang 2012; Ong 1999). For example, what it might mean to be South Asian in America, Australia, Canada, France, Guyana, Malaysia, South Africa, Singapore, Trinidad and Tobago, and many other places where South Asian people are known to reside cannot be taken for granted.

It would also be unfaithful to the reader to suggest that this book provides an all-encompassing account of South Asian girls' and women's engagements with various sport and leisure pastimes.

I pay tribute to others who have done this work from different national and geopolitical contexts and who collectively provide a wider re/presentation than what I have achieved here (e.g., see Ahmad 2011; Chawansky and Mitra 2015; Lenneis and Agergaard 2018; Mani and Krishnamurthy 2016, 2018; Mitra 2009; Nanayakkara 2012; Rana 2017; Samie 2013; Samie and Sehlikoglu 2015; Samie et al. 2015; Shahzadi 2018; Szto 2020). I am mindful, therefore, across the different chapters of this book not to produce essentializing accounts about "all" South Asian girls and women, recognizing that our lived realities across time and space might be structured similarly and differently (Brah 1996)—moreover, acknowledging that my own place "in" this written narrative consciously and subconsciously situates and prioritizes a *British* Asianness and/or Indianness. To this end, I specifically use the concepts of family and friends to illustrate the dynamics of race, gender, and nation from the lived perspectives of British Asian girls and women as they engage in various sport and leisure pastimes.

A Nation of Family and Friends?

Introduction

A Sporting Nation of Family and Friends?

This book is a collection of essays inspired by my research at the intersections of race, gender, and the nation. It privileges sport (and leisure) as a critical window onto a world (James 2013; see also Hartmann 2003) to understand not only how ideas about race and gender are read in and through moving bodies (in this case, the bodies of British Asian girls and women) but, moreover, how everyday engagement with forms of sport and physical activity, as a leisure practice, fosters inclusive and exclusive communities of being and belonging. The stories that emerge about British Asian girls and women, therefore, also represent how they view and position their affinities and/or disunities to the nation (read: England). More specifically, the essays that constitute this collection aim to capture the complex conjunctural context that shapes and is shaped by British Asian girls and women as they navigate various sport and leisure contexts as active agents in their own lives and realities.

This book also speaks to my embodied perspective, acknowledging how I see and make sense of the social world: my lived politics. As I detail in the preface, this sensibility often returns me to thoughts and feelings about my own family and friends and, concomitantly, inspires how I see and read the interpellations of race, gender, and nation. While I move back and forth between my ontological reality (as articulated through the poetry, prose, and manifestos that constitute the interlude and epilogue sections included in this collection), the re/presentations I offer about British Asian girls and women in and through each chapter focus on a particular reading of sport and leisure pastimes. For example, chapter 2 is about the walking pastimes of older British Asian women (sixty to seventy years old at the time of the study), chapter 3 provides gendered analyses of two sporting films focusing on British Asians and football, and chapter 4 is based on the testimonies of second- to third-generation British Asian girls and women (fourteen to forty years old at the time of interviewing them for my doctoral study) about their experiences as football fans and players of the game. Thus, sections of this book can be read as stand-alone chapters and/or in sequential order.

In this introductory chapter, I interrogate friendship further as a means to see and know the social world, especially to view sport and leisure spaces as (physical and imaginary) sites of commons. To begin with, I suggest why a focus on friends, family, and the commons is crucial, in this contemporary #SayHerName moment, to bring people together in solidarity and action rather than to accept social exclusion, discrimination, and isolation. In other words, I start the chapter by recognizing the imbrication of racism and sexism as an omnipresent reality in and beyond the sporting sphere. Despite this reality, I seek to reimagine sport and leisure contexts as also holding liberatory potential. To make this argument, I draw on a range of Black, queer, and Chicana feminist critiques—including the work of Gloria Anzaldúa, Marquis Bey, Kimberlé Crenshaw, María Lugones, and José Muñoz—to argue for sport as a future utopian space. I make this argument knowing sport and leisure sites involve openings (liberatory potential) and closings (discriminatory and exclusionary forces) that are not easily reconcilable and, as debated below, require much work to bring people together through loving perception, radical action, and hope.

Black women's liberation as both feminist and antiracist actors has long been the focus of legal scholar Kimberlé Crenshaw's writings and activisms. Through her 2014 slogan #SayHerName, Crenshaw urges us to call out anti-Black violence in the United States, structured as it is through gendered *and* White supremacist machinations of the police, media, education, and the judiciary, for instance. She, with others, provides a harrowing reminder that Black women are dehumanized in and through police violence (Crenshaw et al. 2015), and this is a routine feature of their everyday lives and realities. Stanley Thangaraj's (2017) statement on the social media site Tropics of Meta lists a wide array of women of color whose sporting lives also have been shaped through complex manifestations of racial, sexual, gendered, nationalistic, neoliberal, and ideological forms of violence and control (see also Brown, *Say Her Name* [forthcoming]). While this symbolic violence does not necessarily lead to them dying, it is nonetheless dehumanizing. This debasement has had a long and symbolically violent history (Crenshaw 1989; McKittrick 2015; Sharpe 2016) that continues to inspire Black, queer, and crip feminist theorizing and activisms within the sphere of sport and leisure studies (e.g., Brown 2022; Carter-Francique and Olushola 2016; Carter-Francique and Richardson 2016; Finney and Mapp 2014; Mowatt, French, and Malebranche 2013; Kuppan 2018; Rallins 2022; Razack 2022; Razack and Joseph 2020; Stanley 2020).

Yet while we must continue to #SayHerName, we must also recognize that this mediated campaign is unrepresentative of the violence experienced by *all* people of color in the United States (Lowe 2015). As further argued by Thangaraj, Arnaldo, and Chin (2016), the sporting desires, pleasures, and advocacy of Asian Americans, for instance, are made invisible through academic, public, and political discourses that predominantly frame debates about the nation (specifically in the United States) through Black-White racial binaries (see also Lowe 2015; Thangaraj 2012; Yep 2012). Indigenous, diasporic, and new migrant rights as well as the politics of colorism must be considered too, as they further complicate debates about race, gender, and the nation (Brown 2017; Jamieson 1998; Razack and Joseph 2020; King 2014; McGuire-Adams 2019; Thangaraj 2022). This, however, is not a straightforward task. As I will demonstrate through the different chapters of this book, this is because spaces of sport and leisure can be experienced as unifying or representative of what Gilroy (2004) terms multicultural conviviality: learning to live (and play) across (social) differences. Embedded within the notion of sport as unifying, the view that sport can create "blud" between those who are not blood related, deepening friendships through shared experience, is common. Yet beyond idealistic notions of friends and family (see the preface), we know such relationships are politically fraught imaginaries, pitting different groups of people against one another—for example, as "good" and "bad" family members, friends, and neighbors (Chatterjee 2021; Montegary 2018; Puar 2007; Ratna 2019; Simpson 2016; Thangaraj et al. 2018; Tillmann 2015; Yuval-Davis, Wemyss, and Cassidy 2018). We also know through the work of many scholars (see above) that the social construction of family often is connected to wider debates about state-endorsed ideals about the nation—who belongs and who does not. Despite this problem, as an analytical and organizing tool, the notion of family and friends still has political worth.

Friendship has long been the scholarly occupation of social philosophers such as Aristotle and Derrida as well as feminists (e.g., Hannah Arendt) and postcolonialists (e.g., Rabindranath Tagore and Leela Gandhi). At a basic level of analysis, moving beyond an understanding of friendship as a site of pleasure (Aristotle) and/or a male preserve (Derrida), exploring friendship as a site of knowing one another has also been recognized as a site for coalition building (e.g., see Banerjea et al. 2018; Çidam 2017; Collins 2012; Davies 2017; Hoare 2018; Laursen 2019; Schneider 2019; Tillmann 2015; Whittaker 2011). As Audre Lorde ([1984] 2007, 56) describes, "The sharing of joy, whether physical, emotional, psychic, or intellectual, forms a bridge between the sharers which can be the basis for understanding much of what is not shared between them, and lessens the threat of difference."

Lessening the threat of difference and building emotional sinews that connect people across time and space can have important healing powers. In this #SayHerName moment, the need for such collective care has never felt greater. Moreover, identifying sport and leisure as a site of commons for fostering collective care is also an invitation to (re)politicize a space that is often viewed as trivial and apolitical (Carrington 2012; Hartmann 2003). This book centers the notion of a sporting or leisure commons (see below) to add to debates about the social proclivities of such spaces for uniting friends, families, and communities of people (i.e., strangers) across social differences and the physical and imaginary boundaries that separate connected land, people, and cultures (Amin 2012; Anzaldúa 1987; de Jong, Icaza, and Rutazibwa 2018; Mignolo 2000; Simpson 2016; Smith 1999; Tuck and Yang 2014). In other words, I question whether sport and leisure spaces can be imagined as utopian future spaces (Muñoz 2009) that transcend discrimination, prejudice, and inequalities to forge new spaces that are deemed "inclusive." Mindful of Simpson's (2016) condemnation of "justice"—as mobilized through state-based neoliberal decolonial projects—how "inclusion" is experienced, and by who, is contingent and contested.

Sport and Leisure as Sites of Playful Commons

A sociology of the commons—as a place of belonging, being, and becoming—often reflects the post-Marxist goals of scholars who grapple with the consciousnesses, needs, and histories of working-class communities to view how economic and cultural resources can be used to end capitalism (and connected racial inequities) and to create new and alternative sites of being and belonging (Amin 2012; Bhattacharya 2018; Bhattacharya et al. 2021; Emejulu 2022; Sivanandan 2008; Virdee 2014). Yet not all of those who share class identities are likely to work together for a common purpose.

The commons, therefore, is not a rigid/fixed social or spatial entity but, as debated by Sobande and Basu (2023), an imaginary, shape-shifting space of belonging and political activism. Acknowledging that social "cliques" can dominate space and resources even from within antidiscriminatory settings, it can feel as if the possibilities for emancipation are limited. As the Black Lives Matter campaign demonstrates, however, spaces of sport and leisure can have the affective power to link players, fans, and different groups of people together through *communing actions* to challenge racism (Sobande and Basu 2023). The socialist vision for cultural spaces, including those of sport and leisure, is hopeful (see below): alliances and closures can coexist, and the *act* of communing can engender conciliatory forces that bring people together (e.g., see also Finney and Mapp 2014; Jackson 2020; Neal et al. 2019; Rallins 2022; Razack 2022; Stanley 2020; Tillmann 2015). To develop this idea further, I turn to Chicana feminist insights.

Commons is a term deployed in many Chicana/o critiques that recognize what Gloria Anzaldúa (1987) would view as "border" work—that is, seeing in and between the borders and divisions of space and identity to make possible new communities of being and belonging. She argues that this does not necessarily mean that the life goals of different members of a community are the same or that identity politics are not relevant to recognizing differential experiences of discrimination. I am further taken by Anzaldúa's (1987) conception of Mestiza to recognize the ambiguous and contradictory positions that women hold across different spaces, including the White male, middle class, heterosexual, and nondisabled spaces of sport and leisure (see Jamieson 1998, 2003; Jamieson and Choi 2017). The concept of Mestiza, therefore, belies any fixed notion of belonging and being. This analysis is crucial to understanding how borders, including those within the spaces of sport and leisure, enable "us" to stand together in difference, knowing that sharing and acting with others can nevertheless still be a productive space of knowing *and* a site of resistance (Jamieson 2003).

Chicana feminist María Lugones (2003) further positions sport and leisure cultures as embodying *play* not in terms of a verb or action but in terms of a noun or essence—in other words, a state of being that enables us to feel a level of emotional intensity to others. This coming together in play allows for a "loving perception"; we "see" others within our own being, recognizing connections and not just differences. This kind of physical, social, and emotional journey is risky, as "play" through competitive forms of sport also involves winners and losers and thus has the potential to evoke hostility. Lugones (2003), returning to Huizinga's work on play as a sociological insight into the intrinsic values of "doing" sport, suggests that playfulness is a joyful, pleasurable, and connective sinew that bonds strangers, friends, and family members, creating long-lasting feelings of "deep" connection (see the preface; Lorde [1984] 2007; Razack 2022). Arguably, sport as a part of leisure (and to a certain extent, elite and competitive sport too) still holds the potential for play, bonding people in a spirit of love, joy, and hope despite the increasingly global, capito-patriarchal governance of modern sports.

Pointedly, Lugones (2003) states that world traveling cannot be a middle-class, leisurely journey to far-off places to consume "the exotic" or an imperial or colonial journey that is agonistic in intention. For her, this is not compatible with the spirit of playfulness, which provides openings for us to travel (metaphorically, spiritually, and physically) to one another as humans, family, friends, and strangers. Lugones (2003, 96) recognizes that "the openness to risk the ground that constructs us as oppressors or as oppressed or as collaborating or colluding with oppression" paves the way for producing deeper knowledge about the complexities of both power and inequity. It involves action and choice to exist in this space differently through loving rather than arrogant perceptions (Lugones 2003).

Lugones (2003), indeed, urges us as scholars and people to make the "loving" journey across social divides (and spaces) and to leave our "arrogant perceptions" behind us to be able to interact "playfully" with those we know or may not know, to generate knowledge about what connects us as humans and as people. In playfulness, arguably, spaces of sport and leisure provide such an opportunity to unlearn privileges (or our own entrenched "arrogant perceptions") and to relearn, from one another, the conditions that connect us across spaces and sites of difference.

Reimagining a Sporting Utopia

As Lugones (2003) further suggests, different social institutions—including the judiciary, sport, education, and the media, for example—often endorse antidiscriminatory stances while concomitantly failing to make themselves more equitable (Ahmed 2006). This recognizes, as many scholars have highlighted (e.g., Bey 2019; Lowe 2015; Montegary 2018; Puar 2007), that despite such institutional gestures, the life chances of racial and ethnic minority men and women continue to be structured in complex and discriminatory ways. In my efforts to grapple with these contradictions and complexities, I have come to value Marquis Bey's radical Black feminist and queer exploration of "them goon rules" as a type of "play." The goon in Bey's work personifies a playful character, or perhaps even a fool, who dares to dream, imagine, and re-create a different place of being and belonging that defies fixed social categorizations and challenges inequities through planned action (see also Harney and Moten 2013).

Developing Bey's appropriation of the "goon," I am also struck by the loving possibilities of organizing and planning together, with others, in/under/at the edges of different institutions and systems of power (Santa Cruz Feminist of Color Collective 2014; see also McGuire et al. 2022; Ratna et al. 2017) as fugitives (i.e., a trespasser, outlaw, undesired, nonbelonger) to *lawfully* activate "real" social change. Fed up with the nonperformance of antidiscrimination in sport, leisure, and higher education, including as it relates to #SayHerName (Ahmed 2006; see also Caudwell, Healy, and Ratna 2023), I believe we urgently need lawful acts of fugitivity to enact social change to make a "real" difference in those structural and cultural contexts (Bey 2019; Kennedy 2019; Harney and Moten 2013; Emejulu 2022). However, like Emejulu (2022), I ponder what this future might look like. Arguably, sport as a form of leisure holds that potential for social change *because* it enables playful connections to one another. That is, it can be experienced as utopian because the pleasure of being together, with others, through playful social encounters creates the conditions conducive to planning a future still in the making.

Muñoz further depicts the utopian possibilities of leisure spaces in relation to his analysis of the U.S. gay dance scene. Specifically, in his text *Cruising Utopia*, Muñoz captures the embodied "freedom" experienced by gay men as they cruise public spaces to partake in sex acts that reconnect them to their bodies and senses of self. During the AIDS epidemic in the 1980s, pushing public sex acts into private spaces for many gay men not only was dangerous but also limited the possibilities of knowing the sexual body as something other than in the closet or as a dying body. Such public spaces of leisure are therefore interpreted as open to utopian possibilities. Muñoz (2009, 66) writes, "In my analysis that does not mean that queers become one nation under a groove once we hit the dancefloor. I am in fact interested in the persistent variables of difference and inequity that follow us from queer communities to the dance floor, but *I am nonetheless interested in the ways in which a certain queer communal logic overwhelms practices of individual identity. I am also interested in the way the state responds to the communal becoming*" (emphasis added).

Arguably, across a range of leisure and sport spaces, those involved (at various levels of engagement) often discuss the unifying nature of such leisure spaces (across markers of individual difference), especially as juxtaposed with the mundane realities of work (see also chapter 2). Yet this perspective does not always capture a contradictory understanding of leisure as a site of division. For example, the importance of peripheral gay spaces for non-White men emerged because they did not fit the blond, muscled, and unavailable sexual bodies of White men who tended to predominate the mainstream New York dance scene (Ferguson 2003; Manalansan 2003; Muñoz 2009). Without losing sight of the utopian possibilities of being in a space at a moment in time, larger social forces penetrate all social relations and leave powerful traditions that, for some, represent a dystopia: a hell rather than heaven on earth. Even from within such spaces of contradiction, like Muñoz (2009), I still hold on to the politics of hope—that is, of a utopian future space. In this present epoch, much political work needs to be done in and through our scholarly praxis to expand our capacities to reimagine how this better world can be constructed and achieved (see also Hall, Massey, and Rustin 2015).

Using the Erotic

Part of the project of creating social change is to consider how the world is read and seen and whose viewpoint is hegemonic. Sociological "classics" such as Wright-Mills's work about using our sociological imaginations have become important introductions to how we know "truths" about this world but, ironically, do not shift the sociological canon to places outside of a Western, Eurocentric, and imperial purview (Amos and Parmar 1984; Bhambra 2014, 2007). Surely, "seeing" the world anew and from a different perspective is also an invitation to consider other systems of knowing outside of and separate from the Western/European canon. I am particularly inspired by Linda Tuhwui Smith (1999), who proposes an antiacademic lens and values "being" as a significant source of knowing the social world. Drawing on my own heritage, as a British Asian woman, I have constructed and included interludes between the more traditional chapters of this book to position and explore my erotic—that is, my embodied, personal, and political values—as a way of knowing (Gupta and Ferguson 1992; Lugones 2003; Lorde [1984] 2007). These interludes serve as a "brave space" (Anzaldúa 1987; McGuire-Adams 2019), knowing public visibility also invites personal and scholarly (over)scrutiny. Yet all sociological perspectives are not and never can be neutral (see also Joseph 2017). I make my private self public (see Ratna 2018) as a reflexive act to make explicit how I make sense of the world from my place within it. Joseph (2017) also uses the erotic to provide thick ethnographic research about race, diaspora, and gender relations and to argue that denying the sensual and sexual elements of research makes for impoverished analyses, which do justice to neither the researcher nor the researched. I agree that making the private self public, as Joseph does, acknowledges how her gender and sexual presence not only enabled the research approach but also unpicked gendered intricacies relevant to capturing a more nuanced and complex appreciation of the Black, sporting, Caribbean diaspora.

I recognize the task of making the private self public is also a strategy to learn, unlearn, and relearn about my own sociological blind spots, discriminatory thinking, and actions (see Ratna 2017a). None of us are holier than thou after all. I undertake this reflexive process to develop a deeper insight into what shapes *my* "seeing," knowing this may also be useful to other scholars to understand meaning-making practices. However, these reflections also stimulate anger. Based on the insights of Lorde ([1984] 2007), I have written before about using anger as a clarifying act of knowing and speaking to the operation of social in/equities—that is, to use my erotic as an embodied form of knowledge production (Ratna 2017c), even if not in my own tongue, to speak without refrain as someone who is not meant to survive the weight of academic Whiteness.

Since writing those words (i.e., Ratna 2017c), I also have come to feel the "rage" that Lugones (2003, 103–118) writes about, the type of fury that is "hard-to-handle anger." Like Lugones, I feel exasperated that I have become the stereotypical "angry woman"— too emotional, rash, and lacking control—rather than the "professional" White academic who speaks about in/justice from a relatively cool place of detachment. Even though I know anger is a rational response to circumstances that induce such vexations, I hate myself for not being able to "turn it off" (or on) as the situation requires. In moments of rage, I feel completely overwhelmed with the emotional reaction to the pain I see, hear, and experience. During these times, I try to take solace in the words of both Lorde ([1984] 2007) and Lugones (2003), noticing that the clarity of my vision through anger and/or rage often lucidly captures the crux of an issue.

I wonder why I still feel surprised by my own ability to produce such critical insights. Perhaps it is because I was told by powerful gatekeepers of this space at the start of my master's and postgraduate education (in the neoliberal university machine that is higher education in the Global North) that I lacked knowledge or, more precisely, that I was not able to translate my lived insights into knowledge that could "pass" through the White, Western, Eurocentric, androcentric, and secular traditions symbolic of higher education. When I speak to the things in my head, knowing from "being" before it was made supposedly "critical" in the academy, it feels real and "true" (see also Smith 1999). Speaking in rage is also a demand, inviting a response (respond, damn it). Seeing myself through the oppressor's eyes, I feel chastised for not controlling such emotions. I am frustrated that I cannot transcend this internal conflict, so I am choosing to embrace it, residing as I always have as an outsider within academia (Ratna 2017c; see also Collins 2000), unleashing the erotic to capture through the juxtaposition of academic prose, poetry, and manifesto writing (see the epilogue) the operations of complex inequities.

I also take to heart the critical insights of Iimonen (2019, 13), who argues that expressing the joint operation of interlocking oppressions cannot necessarily be achieved through "academic intersectionality"—that is, a form of intersectional writing that appropriates intersectional theory without valuing the creative writing (e.g., fiction, prose, poetry) that gives Black feminism its power. As this book has come together, I also have come to see that the interludes and epilogue I have crafted also serve another purpose: to play the trickster, coyote, or goon (Bey 2019; Iimonen 2019) to express the emotional effects of oppression that cannot necessarily be captured through academic prose alone.

Even though I choose to use my erotic and recognize the pleasure and pain of writing from this perspective, I invite White men and women to share the burden of making the private self public (Ratna 2018) in a move to acknowledge the Whiteness that circumscribes our respective and differentiated social beings of work and life (Frankenberg 1993; King 2008; McDonald 2009;

and Watson and Scraton 2001). Social identities must be critically explored to expose colonial, imperialistic, patriarchal, and capitalist regimes of power and control. Despite the long history of discrediting racial and gendered biological myths, institutionalized structures of Whiteness, including in sport and leisure, continue to position racial and ethnic minority groups as always and already inferior to the assumed innate superiority of White Western men and women (Grewal 1996; Emejulu 2022; Lorde [1984] 2007; Saad 2020). As I have written with others elsewhere (e.g., see Thangaraj et al. 2018), the rise of neonationalist politics can also be understood as a re-Whitening project to reproduce and further delineate those who belong within the nation and those who, invariably, do not. This is evident in the way that the mainstream movement of neonationalist politics across both the political right and center positions White communities as "the left-behinds" who are marginalized by political actions to appease racial minority groups. This viewpoint simultaneously positions Whiteness as a social heritage that increasingly lacks power and erases a wider history of Indigeneity, cultural and ethnic diversity, and other systems of meaning across spiritual-human-animal-environmental life worlds (Tuck and Yang 2012).

Whiteness as a process that normalizes structural arrangements and traditions that inherently benefit White communities of people is also evident in the colonial construction of sport as a social space where racial politics are made and remade (Carrington 2010). I would add, moreover, that these are predominantly remade in the image of White (heterosexual) men (Kyeremeh 2019). As I begin this book, to reimagine sociology through the erotic, I want to know who will come and "play" (see also Kumm and Johnson 2018; Ratna et al. 2017)—to join the dialogue as a way of knowing (and loving) one another across our differences as "blud" and not just "blood."

Book Overview

This book includes personal insights, vignettes, and interludes as links in and between the more traditional chapters. I use autobiographical vignettes not only to challenge regimes of knowing and doing sociology (Smith 1999) but also to invite other sociologists to participate in deeper dialogues about what shapes their seeing. This is my erotic, and I want to expose the "darkness" of White supremacist structures and cultures (see interlude 3) as they manifest in spaces of higher education and studies of sport and leisure while also somewhat contradictorily arguing for a space of sport and leisure commons as a future utopian space—more specifically, by exploring the lived leisure and sporting practices of British Asian girls and women.

In chapter 1, I review postcolonial knowledges that explain the lasting legacies of how we come to know the "South Asian woman" over time and space. From the historical deconstruction and reconstruction of the "South Asian woman," implications for exploring their engagements in sport and leisure pastimes are debated. Mainly, I lay out the fallacies of past sporting literatures that rarely move beyond dominant religious and cultural scripts about South Asian femininity. By unpicking these sporting narratives, I (re)demand the need for a more complex, polymorphous, and dynamic understanding of their relationships to sport and leisure cultures (see also Ratna 2018; Ratna and Samie 2017).

Interlude 1 is based on several vignettes capturing my own socialization in the contested spaces of both sport and higher education in the United Kingdom, also using references to popular culture and music to locate the political, social, and economic context that shapes my worldview as a British Asian woman. As I move between time and space, the vignettes serve as an introspective device to bring to the fore what shapes my seeing (van Ingen 2013). While, at times, this felt like an overly self-indulgent process of demonstrating my supposed scholarly virtues, I wish to invite readers to look through these stories to understand how I am "owning" my scholarship by revealing what frames (and does not frame) my seeing.

In chapter 2, I trace first-generation British Gujarati Asian women's historical relationships to public spaces of work to also explore their leisure lives. Significantly, I use the testimonies of these women—including that of my mother, Kesar, and her friends—to think through the gendered, class, and caste dynamics of citizenship and belonging (Ong 1999). The chapter also interrogates how I approached research about my family and friends, providing a gendered critique about the purpose of including both my mother and father as participants and coresearchers, respectively. These methodological choices demonstrate my commitment to challenging androcentric and ethnocentric/Eurocentric, positivistic, colonial legacies and hierarchies, returning to key questions about ontology (the nature of being) and epistemology (how we know). The chapter is a testament to the radical, skilled, and agentic powers of South Asian women to traverse spaces of home and work across time and space as transnational and middle-class *British* citizens while concomitantly demonstrating their ability to resist wider oppressive scripts about class, gender, religion, and belonging.

Further developing understandings of home and belonging for these British Gujarati Asian (specifically Indian) women, in interlude 2, I return to the deadly context of the post-Brexit, populist, and COVID-19 moment, rethinking the changing complexities of belonging and identity formation for my mother and father's walking group. Through this interlude, I also share new empirical materials that emerged from the walking project (chapter 2) to demonstrate how a medical and health rationale reconstructs the diasporic dream of returning "home" to the Indian subcontinent as a fantasy (Brah 1996). I also think about the stories that are not told about "home," family, and friendship—"shaming" stories, specifically about mental health and not just physical health.

Chapter 3 focuses on the filmic representations of British Asian men and women football players. The context of football is important to signal here, not only as the national sport of England, but also because sports like football have often been popularly perceived as having the capacity to unite people and communities across social differences (see also chapter 4). Through a cross-cultural comparison of the British box office hit *Bend It like Beckham* and the Hindi language, London-based, Bollywood film *Dhan Dhana Dhan Goal*, I revisit the significance of sporting spaces as unifying (and diasporic) and also draw out what remains invisible across both films in terms of the interpellations of race, gender, sexuality, and nation: the roles of South Asian women. The juxtaposition and circulation of ideas about the South Asian diaspora (albeit in the Global North) enabled a combined reading of the "view from the West" (through the director Gurinder Chadha's production choices) and a "view from elsewhere" (through Vivek Agnotri's directive choices from "home" within the Indian subcontinent). Friendship and family, debatably, are important concepts that can be applied across both filmic representations to further explore diaspora space—that is, the tension between "home" and "home away from home."

Interlude 3 is based on an interlinked series of poems about my views of higher education in the United Kingdom. These poems express my dissatisfaction with higher education as a site of knowing and being that, for me, is experienced as the "heartness of darkness": a dystopian social reality. Initially read as part of a conference presentation, this interlude describes having to exist as a fugitive in higher education and how it is tantamount to always being Other. The play on words is also a reference to Joseph Conrad's fictional book *Heart of Darkness* (1899), which speaks to the colonial and European fear (and desire) of the Black person in the supposed "heart of darkness": the African subcontinent. The insights from this interlude are not separate from the readings of sport and leisure offered across the different chapters of the book; they express how and why I produce the narratives that I do to show the parallels (and differences) between my experience of higher education, on the one hand, and the sporting experience of other British Asian women in and through various sport and leisure settings, on the other hand.

The racial and gendered context of British Asian Others within the White spaces of women's football is explored in chapter 4. In this chapter, I show the coalescing and conflicting possibilities of belonging in a space that is gendered to probe wider debates about race, nation, class, caste, religion, sexuality, and citizenship. Four key areas are specifically developed: (1) the politics of being a young British Muslim woman representing the United Kingdom at the Islamic Women's World Games, (2) the politics of embodying a rude gal style, (3) individual and collective power, and (4) the convivial nature of football fandom. Critically, this chapter speaks to the politics of multicultural conviviality that recognizes sport as a commons: bringing together people across markers of race, ethnicity, faith, gender, and class.

The concluding chapter reconstructs how British Asian (predominantly Indian) women's engagements in sport and leisure can be read and made knowable as multifaceted, complex, and dynamic. I seek to provide insight into their lives, politics, and pleasures across generational, age, racial, ethnic, class and caste, gender, and sexual differences. Returning to the notion of family and friends, based on the findings that emerged from the empirical and cultural analysis, I evaluate sport and/or leisure spaces as a site of commons to consider the problems and possibilities of working together to survive and to create new and different social worlds that imbue hope and foster a more inclusive space of being and belonging.

In the epilogue, I adopt a rather tongue-in-cheek style. My ambition is to capture how our future research endeavors as scholars of sport and leisure can move beyond the limitations of White, Western, Eurocentric, androcentric, and secular forms of knowledge production. The "heaviness" of this text in places—for me, at least—demanded respite, a lightness. As "I'm not your exotic" (thank you, Urooj Shahzadi, for sharing those words with me at a North American Society for the Sociology of Sport conference in 2015), I refuse to partake in (or disidentify from; see Jamieson and Choi 2017) the supposed "professional" standards (of writing academically) or behaviors (speaking with the "right" academic tone; see Ahmed 2021) that are, to me, essentially oppressive "bullshit" (Littler and Emejulu 2019; see also Ratna 2017c). When I initially wrote this epilogue (in 2020), I chose to mock the insidious foolishness that academics sometimes un/intentionally uphold. Those who read the epilogue may indeed see me as the "goon" described above. But by the time I sent this monograph to the publishers (mid-2022), the reality of being an independent scholar rather than a paid institutional employee has been difficult; surviving financially in austere economic times is not a light matter. Thus, I am OK to play the "goon" for my personal relief, knowing my future employment in the neoliberal university (Bhambra, Gebrial, and Kerem Nişancıoğlu 2018) is contingent on meeting predominantly White, male, and elite expectations and that there are risks for not doing so.

Bridging institutionalized academic spaces and writing poetry and prose, I suggest, provides yet another opportunity to see one another (across occupational divides) in loving perception. I still have hope for my academic future, inspired by the communing politics of so many of my peers "in" the job (see, e.g., McGuire-Adams et al. 2022). Thus, the epilogue is also an invitation to see "us" as British Asian women in our fullness, complexity, and diversity—in our becomings beyond overregulating professional and sociological (Eurocentric, ethnocentric, and androcentric) orthodoxies.

Like all my work and musings, ideas percolate in my mind and take shape as life happens (in relation to my family and friends), and perhaps that is the key part of what I want to emphasize: how we know from our similar and different places of socialization, when made public, helps elucidate the dynamics of how we "see" the social world and the impact of this on how we read the sporting and leisure lifestyles of different communities of people. In this case, I explore how my erotic shapes how I read my life story vis-à-vis other British Asian (Indian) women, as a decolonial, Black, and transnational feminist praxis.

Before focusing on an empirical and cultural analysis of materials across chapters 2, 3, and 4, I turn next to chapter 1 to critique how the "South Asian woman" comes to be known through colonial and postcolonial readings. Moreover, I will think through how such predominant representations impact knowledge in the field of sport and leisure studies.

1

The Making of the
"South Asian Woman"

"Who" South Asian women are is a key ontological question that structures the first part of this chapter. I revisit colonial and postcolonial critiques, including the scholarship of Indian diasporic scholars such as Inderpal Grewal (1996), Chandra Talpade Mohanty (1984, 2003), and Gayatri Chakravorty Spivak (1988), to deconstruct how popular images of the "South Asian woman" have come to dominate studies of sport and leisure. As part of this deconstruction, I argue that while "new" iterations of the "South Asian woman" have emerged, the lived subjectivities of South Asian women from across the diaspora remain relatively static. I specifically argue that South Asian women's bodies in postcolonial times have become markers and measures of modernity, through which the multiplicities of South Asian women's "real" lives remain, to various extents, invisible.

From this deconstruction, the second part of the chapter reviews how the dominant image of the "South Asian woman" continues to frame how their sporting engagements are made knowable. I suggest that three key metanarratives have become central: (1) South Asian women are weak and unable to participate in physically demanding sport and leisure pastimes; (2) as heterosexual women, and to maintain familial respectability, they must meet supposed cultural and religious requirements to cover their bodies and behave modestly (read: not to bare flesh or move their bodies in ways that may be depicted as sexually alluring to men); and (3) South Asian women can only ever be made knowable as heterosexual actors. Through the subsequent chapters of the book, I write back to universalizing re/presentations of South Asian femininities to explore further the multifarious, complex, and nuanced relationship that they have with sport and leisure cultures.

Re/presenting the "South Asian Woman"

To write about the long, polymorphous, and complex histories of women from South Asia and their diasporic identities is impossible in one chapter. The question is not necessarily where to begin but how to encompass the multiplicities of South Asian women's lived realities and their ever-changing relationships with the social world. Their viewpoints cover expansive geopolitical terrain in and beyond South Asia (Brah 1996). The act of recovering the genealogies of South Asian women as a heterogeneous group is a political act (Spivak 1988), retracing the historical, social, economic, cultural, and political shifts, complexities, and contradictions that, for me, start with the material and linguistic construction of the "South Asian woman."

Sociological analysis in late modern times focuses on the body to uncover fleshy, sensual, and political knowledges (Grosz 1994). Nevertheless, South Asian women are only ever made knowable through fixed and problematic scientific frames of reference (see above). During colonial times, such scientific tropes worked to position South Asian women as a homogeneous group, biologically weaker than South Asian men and White men and women (Grewal 1996). In sporting and leisure contexts, their supposed physical frailty is read as having two interconnected effects: (1) it explains their lack of engagement in physical activity and (2) it perpetuates their desirability as delicate (meaning: feminine) creatures ripe for "deflowering." Their sexuality, therefore, is (re)produced as nonmasculine, nonbutch, and nonthreatening—that is, the "exotic" Other. Any possibility of knowing the lived embodiments of race, gender, and sexuality for South Asian women remains, as Spivak

(1988) would suggest, "in the shadows" (see Ratna 2017a for further debate).

The colonial legacy of the British Empire, in and across the South Asian region, is often uncritically romanticized to focus only on "positive" outcomes (Grewal 1996; Mohanty 1984, 2003)— for example, replacing the so-called archaic organization of social life and familial arrangements before colonization with Western systems of knowledge and schooling as well as exporting institutions such as those of sport, law, and education. Sports like cricket, for instance, were supposedly used to teach the local population British(er) values and norms (Fletcher 2011), reinforcing, in the process, assumptions about the colonizer as superior in both mind and body (see also Bhambra 2007). British gentlemen playing cricket with their Indian servants reproduced White patriarchal hegemonic arrangements (Amos and Parmar 1984): the Indian men would run between the wickets for the British players, as they were deemed not socially refined and physically competent enough to warrant batting privileges.

Grewal (1996), in her deconstruction of colonial fictions, summates that it would be wrong to assume that women had no part to play in the history of the British Empire. Many upper-class White women supported the colonial project by organizing charitable events, raising money to support troops, and while in the colonies, enjoying the consumption of the "exotic" (food, music, art, and culture) while local populations suffered the loss of their land, rights, and possessions. Though South Asian women were not present on the cricket field of play, this does not mean that their presence was not imbricated through such sporting histories. For instance, sexual narratives historically positioned (upper-class) White British women as chaste and pure (to be protected from the sexually deviant exploits of local South Asian men). In contrast, South Asian women were deemed available for the leisure, pleasure, and sexual comfort of White British soldiers. Many of these soldiers were married and thereby engaging in unchristian behaviors: having adulterous relationships with local South Asian women. In such colonial reconstructions, the sexual appetites of White British men, in comparison to that of South Asian men, were not similarly demonized. The history of South Asian women as leisure "commodities," symbolic objects of White men's pleasure, erased any sense of leisure or pleasure that the women may have experienced and/or desired. The project of retrieving South Asian women's sport and leisure histories, therefore, remains an important objective to not only recover their individual and collective subjectivities but also make visible colonial and gendered fictions.

The "New" Indian Woman

In postcolonial times, after the fall of the British Empire, the circulation of dominant discourses about the South Asian woman continued to travel across the Global North and South. This circulation, frustratingly, did little to challenge colonial fantasies about the South Asian woman. As persuasively argued by Menon (2009), despite attempts to retrieve alternative standpoints and to recognize the complexities of class, caste, gender, and sexuality, monolithic constructions of the South Asian woman are often solidified. Menon (2009) argues that the Indian woman (akin to the South Asian woman) is often positioned as "pure" and "free"—supposedly from the Western, White, and secular obsession with (hetero)sexual attractiveness and the quest for sexual gratification. The "new" Indian woman is thus deemed to exist on a higher moral plane than the "White Western woman" (Abraham 2000; Chandra 2020; Chatterjee 2021; Gopinath 2005)—that is, as a woman choosing to be modest/chaste and devoted to her family, like the mythological figure of the Hindu goddess Sita (Chatterjee 2021; Sharpe 2005; Grewal 1996; Mankekar 1999). By extolling the mythical virtues of Sita, the White Western woman is reframed as essentially "loose"— sexually promiscuous and sex obsessed (Chandra 2020).

The lived realities of sex and sexuality for South Asian women (and White Western women), in this reading, are thereby homogenized (Chandra 2020; Dave 2012). The pervasiveness of Hindu mythology, reproduced through nationalistic politics in places such as India and across the Indian diaspora, is so ubiquitous that notions of womanhood very rarely transcend acceptable frames of how South Asian women's bodies can be seen or read. Indeed, as part of its nationalistic rhetoric, the state often reframes and applies value to Indian women's bodies through modern terms, which ties any analysis of their sexuality to moral codes of religious and cultural virtuousness. This rhetoric recognizes that Indian women are sexual beings and modern agents, on the one hand, and embody respectable femininity—as moral and chaste beings—on the other hand. Through such cultural re/presentations, hegemonic and fixed constructions of the "new" Indian woman become a defining set of social arrangements to view the nation-state more broadly rather than to see Indian women through their lived embodiments and gendered subjectivities more specifically (Grewal 1996).

To retrieve more expansive understandings of South Asian women's life stories, we need to recognize that (1) a strong religious and cultural influence on what is deemed "appropriate" in the study of South Asian women continues to shape the field of knowledge, and (2) we cannot assume that White Western articulations of sexuality respond to South Asian histories, vernaculars, and ontological expressions of sex and sexuality (Phillips et al. 2021; Chandra 2020; Chatterjee 2021; Dave 2012; Gopinath 2018; Khubchandani 2020). Thus, "who" gets to tell their stories is a political matter, as they have the power to control their scripts outside of and separate from colonial, nationalistic, and gendered knowledge production regimes and to make their own re/presentational choices.

Dave's (2012) rich ethnographic accounts of feminist politics within India recognize "who" (which men and women) has access to the political realm and how they use and control the political agenda to reinforce and/or subvert the heteropatriarchal organizational structure of private and public life. The political struggles of men and women positioned as Dalits, for example, signal a history and social context in India where birth and bloodlines are crucial to maintaining familial distinction and political power (see the preface). Biological inferences that position Brahmin heritage as a derivative of Aryan tradition, people, and culture (i.e., akin to Whiteness) are powerful because they account for upper-class and caste superiority, beauty, and purity. In studies about the "new" Indian woman, for example, notions of a casteless society are promulgated, while implicitly, Brahminical viewpoints remain center stage and in/directly marginalize a range of racial and ethnic Others (e.g., Muslims, Dalits, hijras, LGBTQI communities, and non-elite class and caste groups).

In Grewal's (1996) colonial critique wherein she deconstructed the "new" Indian woman, the "real" Indian women who emerged, she rightly points out, were reflective of a minority of elite class and caste women. Even in the sport and leisure literature, for example, selective re/presentations about the conspicuous consumptive lifestyles of more upwardly mobile middle-class women homogenize the experiences of all Indian women (Naganathan, Gupta, and Prasad 2021). Who South Asian women are beyond such controlling and selective nationalistic imaginaries, on their own terms and across markers of class, caste, sexuality, nation, religion, generation, and geographical location, remains relatively unknown.

Sport and South Asian Girls and Women

The image of the physically weak and nonsporting South Asian woman continues to be perpetuated, for example, through Sport England survey statistics. These show that South Asian girls and women in the United Kingdom are the least likely racial and ethnic group to participate regularly in any form of physical activity (Sport England 2021). While it would be interesting to see which spaces and sites Sport England evaluators count in their official representation of participation statistics, arguably, they are not reflective of informal sport settings or dance contexts. These contexts are simply not captured through traditional (mainstream) sport and leisure provision. For example, exercising with friends at local parks or having a game of football in the garden is not included in these statistics (see chapter 4). More significantly, as suggested by Shahzadi (2018) in her research about South Asian women, sport, and physical activity in Canada, statistics fail to capture the reasons why some South Asian women may not want to take part in national and mainstream sport and leisure pastimes.

At the start of the twenty-first century, though, predominant notions that South Asian girls and women are not interested in sport continue to be promulgated. At the same time, South Asian women's elite-level achievements across an array of sporting spaces are, to various extents, recognized (see also chapter 4). Examples include Bala Devi (football), Isa Guha (cricket), Mary Kom (boxing), Smitri Mehra (golf), Sania Mirza (tennis), Shika Tandon (swimming), Aishwarya Pissay (motocross), Karenjeet Kaur Bains (powerlifting), Saina Nehwal (badminton), and Ruqsana Begum (Muay Thai). A former colleague, Saima Hussain, for instance, in 2019–2020, was in training to reach her goal of representing the England Women's Rugby League team (having been previously selected) before an ankle injury (from bouncing too high on the trampoline with her beloved nephews) ended this dream (personal correspondence, January 2020). She continues to play for a local women's rugby league team. Beyond the limitations of colonial logic, often missing from re/presentations of South Asian women's sporting careers are accounts of confident women enacting pride in their diasporic heritages and social locatedness. We rarely hear these types of stories. Instead, what emerges through popular narratives is a single, universalizing story: South Asian girls and women pushed away from a sporting life by archaic religious, cultural, and familial orthodoxies. Many intergenerational studies also reproduce deficit models of analysis, depicting sporting transcendence for South Asian girls and women as predominantly achieved by going against the desires, wishes, and cultural traditions of their parents (see also Abdel-Shehid and Kalman-Lamb 2015). Not only is this outdated narrative insulting to first-generation parents who are passionate sport consumers and participants and whose engagement with physical activity is also evolving (Ratna 2017a); it negates how British-born generations, for instance, are becoming parents who vociferously demand inclusivity and sporting equity (Burdsey and Randhawa 2012).

I also question if South Asian women who compete at elite levels of sport have the freedom to speak forthrightly about their gendered, sexual, and sensual desires and pleasures. Not just because such embodied sensual, sporting, and physical pleasures are often deemed culturally taboo; as young people who are "coming of age," sharing their innermost fears, desires, and sexual proclivities publicly might be both scary and embarrassing. They might be judged by their social peers about "doing" their gender appropriately (Butler 1990; Ratna 2013; Scraton and Watson 1998)—especially, that is, considering the long history of Western sporting cultures that promote the (over)surveillance of women's bodies. Arguably, in a media-dominated, neoliberal, and elite women's sporting industry, many White women may also be reluctant to reveal sexual intimacies and desires to protect their "brand" (Cole and Hribar 1995). In this context, it is not difficult to understand why it might be easier for South Asian girls and women to speak to accepted narratives about South Asian cultural transcendence rather than to call out institutional racism, sexism, and homophobia (see Ratna 2013).

The example of African American tennis player Serena Williams is a case in point: any deviation from normative codes of behavior that may be read as disrupting the Whiteness of women's tennis and/or the racist actions of those in power are likely to result in marginalization and exclusion (see also Razack and Joseph 2020; Tredway 2019). To expose White fragility is to become a point of soreness for those in power (Ahmed 2017; DiAngelo 2019). It is not surprising, therefore, that many sporting women—across their racial, ethnic, gendered, and sexual differences—understand that their success is based on their complicity to dominant gender ideals (Adjepong 2015; Ratna 2013). Even the increase of women in sports predominantly seen as men's sports does not change the system because participating women, at times, come with their own conservative values that reaffirm sporting patriarchy and Whiteness. It is from this representational basis that three interconnected myths continue to position South Asian girls and women as sporting misfits: Brown bodies "out" in the White spaces of sport at both elite and recreational levels of participation. I write back to these interconnected myths to challenge anew how South Asian women have come to be seen and read in and across various sport and leisure literatures (see also Ratna 2018; Ratna and Samie 2017).

Too Weak to Play a Man's Sport? Despite having demonstrated that they are far from the frail, mild, and meek colonial stereotype, South Asian women in the elite context of sport still must negotiate dominant gendered tropes based on scientifically false ideas about sex. In my own research about British Asian girls and women football players in the United Kingdom, most of the interviewed girls and women assert that they are competitive players and that they can play aggressively and be tough (see chapter 4). Notions of appropriate femininity were influential, though, and they understood that to be too strong or masculine in and through their involvement in football was tantamount to "being a man" (Ratna 2013). In similar and different ways, all the British Asian women I spoke to (in 2003–2005), through performative speech acts—what they say and do in terms of both their race and gender—asserted both their heterosexuality and femininity (for further detail, see Ratna 2013). In her study, Samie (2013) found that British Muslim women basketball players enjoyed the sensory and embodied feeling of being strong, powerful, and heterosexy, and this is an empowering aspect of their sporting involvement.

The alternative to accepted performances of heterosexual femininity is to be castigated for "being on drugs" (Ratna 2008): reading the bodies of other women football players as too muscular and/or too butch to be "real" women (Cahn 1994; Caudwell 1999). The success of the Indian athlete Dutee Chand responds to this rhetoric: her femininity was scientifically rendered abnormal even though she grew up as a "girl" and talented athlete (Mitra 2018). While it is not my intention here to unpick the scientific fallacies that underpin the contested use of unfair "sex testing" procedures on athletes such as Chand by the International Olympic Committee (IOC), arguably, racialized and fit bodies are often oversurveyed and depicted through popular and mediated accounts as "nonwomen" (for further debate, see Karkazis and Jordan-Young 2018a; Karkazis and Jordan-Young 2018b).

In the infamous media treatment of the South African runner Caster Semenya, her Black body also was popularly understood as too manly and, thus, a threat to the success and hard-won struggles of White "feminine" women (Karkazis and Jordan-Young 2018a; Karkazis and Jordan-Young 2018b). Arguably, part of erasing Chand's athletic performances is also questionable, as it is contrary to dominant and continuously circulating ideas about Indian women's bodies as physically frail (Ratna 2018). Chand's embodied sense of self remains hidden knowledge, unable as she is to escape the discursive logic that re/produces images of South Asian women (as a whole) as inherently and always physically weak. This prevailing discourse is imperative to continuing to construct the athleticism of White Western women as always and already "naturally" superior and feminine (see also Ratna and Samie 2017).

Inappropriate Femininities. Popular, filmic, and academic re/presentations of South Asian women also often position them as purveyors of assumed moral purity, kindness, and nurturing sensibilities—that is, respectable femininity. The prevalence of gossip cultures and cultural shaming of girls and women who fail to conform to normative expectations of appropriate femininity (which, for South Asian girls and women, is embodied by not displaying sexual impulses and/or other pleasures aroused in/through their bodies) is given cultural importance. In some contexts, those girls and women who are judged by male and/or female guardians as transgressing the boundaries of appropriate femininity may even be excluded from family and kinship networks. Without denying the prevalence of unfair and unequal standards placed on maturing girls and young women to regulate their femininities, to suggest this is a predominantly South Asian cultural issue ignores the ways that White and Western women are also publicly shamed (and excluded from families and friendship circles) because they may be deemed "unladylike" for not having appropriate sexual mores and tastes. For instance, the White English middle-class mother of Jules (short for Juliette) in the film *Bend It like Beckham* comes to mind, chastising her daughter for becoming like "Sporty Spice" (read: lesbian) and, thus, for not having a boyfriend (see interlude 1).

Women across different racial and ethnic class contexts, therefore, are judged in ways that limit their engagement in sporting cultures, where they can be diametrically critiqued for wearing too much clothing (e.g., covering bodies while participating in sport) or not wearing enough (displaying seminaked bodies in sports such as volleyball and gymnastics). These standards fluctuate, depending on the sociocultural and geographic context, from one moment to another. A South Asian woman, for example, covering up on a British beach is read in mediated narratives as evidence of cultural subordination, whereas a White woman wearing only a bikini while playing beach volleyball (during the Olympics in London 2012) is supposedly free. While I use this example as a polarizing demonstration of how gendered narratives of appropriate dress operate for different groups of women, the point is that messages about proper femininity are not even subtle but directly manifest through neoliberal media and marketing logic. Arguably, it is just as possible for South Asian women to express their senses of being fit, healthy, and sexy while their bodies are fully covered as it is for White Western women to feel used, pressured, and embarrassed wearing sporting attire that they feel reveals too much of their bodies. It is my purpose here not to uphold such a binary construction but to signal how this debate masks the elite White male sovereignty of sporting rules, media, and marketing strategies that make these types of re/presentations possible.

South Asian and Straight? One area of academic debate that has been neglected in much of the sporting and leisure literature (my work included) about South Asian girls and women relates to their expressions of sexuality. It is naive to assume that being "South Asian" and "gay" is a contradiction in terms. The queer lives of South Asian men and women are evident in and across spaces of leisure, including film and fiction, where a number of writers/directors are taking up both mainstream and avant-garde re/presentations of queer South Asianness in new and interesting ways (e.g., Khubchandani 2020). I recall being in awe of the collection *Red Threads* (Desai and Sekhon 2003), for example, which included photographic re/presentations of South Asian queer bodies in and across different parts of London, using fashion, style, and attitude in different ways to carve out specifically South Asian "fishyness" (meaning: realness). The authors express this multiplicity as "queer Asian Brits, queens in Bollywood drag, women in men's suits or naked on the streets of Britain" (Desai and Sekhon 2003). At the same conference in London where Desai and Sekhon (2003) launched their book, another scholar, Rani Kawale, presented her research (Kawale 2003) about South Asian gay and lesbian clubbing scenes in London. Querying my own fascination and objectification of Brown, South Asian, queer bodies in the process, I began to appreciate further the somatic pain of being a body "out-of-place" (Puwar 2004). More specifically, being queer in queer-friendly spaces is not necessarily a given for those whose skin color positions them as always and already strange (Kawale 2003). To be Brown—lesbian, gay, transgender, and intersex—sticks out because of the continued presentation of South Asians (including those first- and/or second-generation diasporas) as only ever knowable as passive and/or disloyal "straight" citizens (Puar 2007).

In the twenty-first century, the complex, changing, and lived social expressions of gender and sexuality are evolving and contradictorily depicted in Bollywood and independent film houses, where pre- or postmarital heterosexual relations and lesbian intimacies are being explicitly explored. For instance, in Deepa Mehta's film *Fire*, she evocatively captures the sexual tension and intimacies that grow between two married women who, as sisters-in-law (married to brothers), explore the boundaries of same-sex relationships. These women are not "out" as unrespectable South Asian women but, protected by the sanctity of marriage, "in" at home—that is, the private space of upper-caste and class domesticity. It is the turn to lived, embodied, and discursive sexual ontologies in and across the South Asian diaspora that I suggest is an area of sociological inquiry that remains relatively invisible in studies of sport and leisure. This is because scholars (who may or may not be South Asian or queer) continue to reproduce outdated tropes about South Asian femininity as only ever heterosexual and tied to the domestic without querying how and why public and private spaces are made meaningful by South Asian women as sexual beings in their own lives and histories. What it means to be a South Asian "woman" is therefore positioned as only ever a fixed heterosexual discursive category.

Conclusion

In sum, the "sporting South Asian woman" is visible in/through public, political, and mediated discourses. Alternative re/presentations, however, are made impossible in two ways: (1) through objectifying tales that acknowledge their involvement in sport and leisure pastimes but, nevertheless, "read" them as objects of South Asian patriarchal cultural traditions; and (2) in other studies about women's liberties as a measure and monitor of enlightenment, social progress, and modernity, which fail to consider what it might mean to be a passionate, sporty, and physically active woman of South Asian heritage as separate from nationalistic and patriarchal agendas.

In addition to this, as I have argued elsewhere (Ratna 2018), scholars must question the objectification of women's bodies (White/Western and South Asian) to uncover the subjectivities, embodiments, and material realities of women living at the intersections of race, gender, and nation—to make visible systems of meaning that they themselves apply to their sporting and leisure pastimes, needs, and desires (see also Mashereghi 2021). I argue that the continual focus on culture and religion and/or South Asian women's empowerment often only reinforces hegemonic, White, Western, and colonial narratives that reproduce the South

Asian woman as straight, unsporting, physically incompetent, and passive.

It is time to change the script, to provide a more capacious analysis of South Asian women's engagement in sport and leisure pastimes that do not take for granted complexities of race, ethnicity, gender, class, caste, sexuality, age, generation, and (dis)ability. There are so many more stories to tell, and so many more are still in the making. The chapters that constitute the rest of this book aim to do just that, recognizing, though, that this is still a partial representation of South Asian women's different and diverse engagements in sport and leisure cultures.

INTERLUDE ONE:
ENGAGING MY "EROTIC"

The vignettes included here reflect on how I see the world from my place in it, accounting for both enduring and changing viewpoints and memories from different moments in my life story (so far). The purpose of this reflective exercise is to acknowledge how my lived experience is the basis for how I make sense of the world—the things I see—and also, in relation to this, to expose what I do not see or have missed. It recognizes how *all* scholars, including myself, cannot be separate and "objective" from the realities we are inspired to research and write about in addition to how we write about them and the meanings we extract as a result.

While I had initially selected a few vignettes to introduce my worldview, this did not feel complete. The several vignettes that have now been included make me realize two things: First, the vignettes continue to speak to the lives of my friends and family. They serve as a tool to grapple further with the ideas, concepts, and theories developed in the preface and introduction. Second, I do not wish to elevate my worldview over and above that of other postcolonial, Indigenous, Black, Chicana, postcolonial, and transnational feminist writers, as this would universalize a decolonial approach (my approach) as *the* only way to write back to academic systems of knowledge and control. Such a false move would not only reproduce the problem of universalization (of hegemonic Eurocentric, ethnocentric, androcentric, and secular systems of knowing) as stated by de Jong, Icaza, and Rutazibwa (2018); it would also erase the notion of doing decolonial anti-imperial work as a pluriversal project from the ground up (see also Smith 1999).

I share these vignettes as a means for the reader to deconstruct what frames my seeing (van Ingen 2013) and shapes the interpretations I offer in the different chapters of this book. By sharing these vignettes, I hope to inspire others to make their private selves public (Ratna 2018), knowing, like me, that our respective meaning-making practices can be both capacious and limited (at the same time). This is a call to acknowledge our scholarly "blind spots" (for me, this phrase is apt, as ableness and disabilities are often missed from my reading of the world). In this vein, I offer myself "up," hoping the reader will address any erasures beyond my purview and be kind: please do not eat me up and then spit me out (see hooks 1992), thank you.

"Tell Me What You Want, What You Really, *Really* Want"

I grew up in the United Kingdom in the 1990s, an era announced by media and public commentators as the age of "girl power": "tell me what you want, what you really, really want" was the anthem. Sung by the internationally renowned pop band the Spice Girls, each member of the group embodied different styles, enacting the sentiment that if you want to be a popstar, working professional, fashionista, sporty girl, and cute, you could be, as the power was in your hands to "just do it" (as the famous Nike sporting apparel constantly reminded us through televisual advertising campaigns). During these times, the hedonistic and consumer (credit) culture that dominated the 1990s in the United Kingdom made things seem possible; you could indeed have it all. For many women of my generation (born in the late 1970s), the "girl power" call signified an age of freedom—that is, from the restrictions of domestic life / motherhood and the ability to control our own destinies by getting an education, getting a job, and demanding the kind of sexual liberty that had been enjoyed for far too long by our male peers (Munford and Waters 2014). What a fantasy we (my friends and I) lived; what a fantasy media cultures, advertisers, politicians, and popstars alike had us believe. The voice inside my head, and the feeling deep inside my gut, informed me otherwise: "This is not real." But, alas, mixed with fear and excitement, like many young women of my generation, I fled the parental nest (home) to embark on my university education and adult life. I wish I had listened to my inner voice or what Lorde ([1984] 2007) terms "the erotic" as an embodied source of knowledge and power (see the preface).

"It's [Not] a London Thing"

At the age of sixteen, I felt acutely aware that I lived in a closed space, and from within this space, my options in life were limited. I thought I would live and die in my parental home, which stimulated different feelings, resonating between the safety and comfort of being "in" a known space as well as anxiety that my life aspirations would not come true from within this relatively small abode. From within the local environment, next to the home of the national sport, English football (soccer) at Wembley Arena, I went to my first rave: Ravelation (1995). While often critiqued by the "original" ravers of the summer of love (1988) and those involved in the acid house scene (see Richards 2017), the neoliberal culture that underpinned such "big" commercial raves carried the possibilities of becoming something else or someone else, however temporal that shape-shifting might have been (McRobbie 1991; Redhead 1997). Without wanting to evoke a postmodern assemblage of difference, raver friends and I *felt* unified across signifiers of class, gender, race, and ethnicity. I experienced freedom and a sense of love that my active involvement in sport (a more acceptable subcultural pastime) embodied too. I was less aware at that time of social difference (even though my sister and I were racially bullied at primary school) and reveled through moments of escape from the embodied and doomy subconscious sense of my own (limited) socioeconomic reality (Redhead 1997). Through these formative experiences, I began to see and appreciate sites of leisure (in this case, the U.K. rave/dance scene and spaces of sport) as a "commons": a unifying space.

Becoming "One of the Girls"?

I never drank a pint of lager until I went to university. I blame the netball girls. But who was I going to be, "one of the netball girls," a hockey "posh" one, or one of the lesbian football players? Like the Spice Girls, which one was I prepared to embody as the acceptable "face" of girl power? Early on during my time at university, and after being welcomed by senior members of the netball team so warmly, I chose this group of people to hide among even though my shade of Brownness on a predominantly White team and university context made me anything but invisible. University was a "coming-of-age" time but also pretty crap; I was lonely. I missed home. I did not like being the only "one" who was different and having to account for myself (culturally and religiously) as the first South Asian person most of my peers had ever met. I think I raised curiosity. I became a fascination for other male and female university students. *I am no different from you*, I thought. When I write *you*, I am not sure *who* I am referring to—as I knew some people as friends, lovers, and partners from within this sea of Whiteness. I cannot write any more about this time.

I got out, and I will never go back there again. I understand this pain more so now than I did then. It fueled me to keep working hard and get something out of an unhappy time in my life. Learning, in fact, became a coping mechanism. When things at work (as a university lecturer) start frazzling at the edges, and I am unable to pull them together, I wonder how to cope when the coping mechanism does not work. Pain becomes my friend. I live with it in my body, feel its knot in the base of my tummy (Lorde [1984] 2007), and let go sometimes too—unburden myself through hedonistic pleasures, and also, sometimes, I write again. I accept that mental well-being is an ongoing struggle. I spurn the neoliberal do-gooders who preach "If only she had the determination to 'fix' it"; "What a failed human being she is." (For important reads, see Fullagar and O'Brien 2014; Fullagar, O'Brien, and Pavlidis 2019.) I share this with whoever reads this work, my work: embrace your erotic. This is the passion, pain, and energy that underpins "how" we see the stories we choose to tell and how we go about telling them (Lorde [1984] 2007, Anzaldúa 1987).

"The Book Thief"

My political sensibilities are shaped by not only my lived experiences but the people and "things" that I have been exposed to as I grew up, went to university, and embarked on a career in academia. At the time, not knowing what academia involved and what skills and knowledge were required of me to stay in this profession, reading became a long-term occupation (meaning: an occupation in my life and career). Reading was a learned habit—copied, perhaps, to keep up with friends and school peers. I enjoyed it. Decluttering my bookshelf decades later, I stumbled across the books that I stole (yes, stole) from school cupboards and/or never returned to teachers who gave all students copies of key texts. In my young mind, this thievery was justified. How else would I get copies of books that "touched" me (even if I didn't know how or know where to buy them from even if I could afford them)? I can hear in my head other academics possibly asking, "Is she for real?" "Yes" is my answer. Upon reflection, I view my decisions as a young person as motivated by a class-based reality—no one was going to buy me such books, and I didn't have the cultural, social, and economic capital to buy them for myself.

This is how I have come to have copies of books such as *The Duchess of Malfi*, *Poetry of the 30s*, *Henry V*, *The Labour of Keir Hardie*, and *Our Lives*, to name a few. Many of these books opened the world to me from my corner of northwest London in the late 1990s, when I really began to think about power, status, marginalization, and discrimination. I despised the text we had to read for a General Certificate of Secondary Education (GCSE) physical education qualification: *Tom Brown's School Days*. I did not like the school prefect system; I found it elitist and bullyish. It reminded me of the playground politics operating in my own school that decided which girls were popular (meaning: most attractive to the male heterosexual gaze, which, despite the diverse racial and ethnic composition of the boys in my year, was implicitly understood as being any of the White girls). The sporty group were all made prefects and had access to special sixth-form facilities and spaces, students studying "lesser" postsixteen courses did their own thing in the "B" Block, and young men and women who were too geeky to be cool and/or were perceived as potentially gay were teased. My sixteen-year-old self wondered about these dynamic fissures.

I was reading other books too, introduced to me by my English teacher, that grappled with complexities of social deprivation (Charles Dickens's *Hard Times*), sexual freedom and pleasure for women (*The Wife of Bath*), and racial injustices (Harper Lee's *To Kill a Mockingbird*). The latter book has had a long-lasting impact on how I see the world, or what Lee described as "stepping into the skin of someone else and walking around in it."

Other books also caught my attention: Salman Rushdie's *The Satanic Verses*. I feel ashamed now that I enjoyed reading this book. Triggered by the scenes of the book burning on the streets of Bradford and Ayatollah Khomeini issuing a fatwa on Salman Rushdie's head, I did not understand at the time why Muslims across the United Kingdom and beyond were outraged, and moreover, I did not see my own complicity in demonizing discourses about Muslim Others from my "lofty" status as a British-born Gujarati and self-defined liberal Hindu person. Owning this perception now really grates on my sense of self. The book added to the already heightened tensions in and across the United Kingdom in the 1980s following the violent stabbing of several British Muslim boys and the conviction of the Bradford Twelve (who were making Molotov cocktails to defend themselves from ongoing neofascist attacks in their local towns and cities, often with little support from the police). This reality collided in a project I began in 2007 (post-PhD) about British Pakistani Muslim cricket players from the northeast of England when one of the participants reflected on being "one" of the Bradford Twelve and his views since that time on the social world and the role of sport in general and cricket in particular (see Ratna, Lawrence, and Partington 2015 for further detail). It is an important lesson for us all—the ongoing challenge of un/learning and re/learning social inequalities by "stepping into the skin" of others and walking around in it to see life from different perspectives. Lugones (2003; see the preface) might call this a form of "loving perception."

"Smelling" the Political Context

It was my university friend Nicola who introduced me to a fictional text written by the eminent Indian author and activist Arundhati Roy and her wonderfully rich book *The God of Small Things*. Here started a long-term affinity with her political writings about India, women's rights, class and caste-based issues, and global manifestations of power and control. And as a follower of her life story, I received the comfort of knowing that an Indian divorcée can live and thrive as a public intellectual. Yet her iconicity inside and outside of India is not a given, as I found out from an uncle in India who suggested my sister and I were "misguided" Westerners who followed Roy but had no concept of what change in India *really* involved. This Hindu political commentator, a local journalist, meant we did not appreciate the "cost" of social progress in India. Outliers in India but of Indian heritage, "know-it-all" young Western upstarts who did not live in the country we were passionately speaking to and about. He is right, isn't he? Even in India, many others do not attach a revered status to an elite class and caste woman, as her writing is about "them" but not "owned" by "them" as narrators of their own life stories. These thoughts (my internal dialogue) are important to lay down, as they frame my view of who has the power to control the script and, perhaps, signal our responsibilities as engaged readers to read "off" the script—that is, to ask other types of questions about how ideas and images of people travel to where, to whom, and for what purpose.

In 2019, I went to a book reading where Arundhati Roy read sections from her second fictional novel, *The Ministry of Utmost Happiness* (2017), since the release of her Booker Prize winner *The God of Small Things* (1997). The book that never stops giving. I wanted to tell Roy that I "smelled" Kerala when I read her book. That I was traumatized by the sticky-lemon sherbet man who made Rahel do that thing. That I asked myself questions such as "Who were the naxalites?" and "Should I support their cause in a real-life context?" and "What does it mean to be of Christian faith (and closer to Whiteness) in a religious and cultural velodrome (that made me feel dizzy when I went with my parents on religious pilgrimages in India as a young person) where historical caste scripts dictate who you can love, and how much?" The history of things matters, and Roy brings this into beautiful, stark, and unflinching reality. Can words make you smell? Can they? Is that an embodied way of knowing a place far from where I am sat now (in Leeds, north of England, at 8:50 p.m. on the fifteenth of May, into week nine of "lockdown" life)? Traveling cultures: a book that has traveled across time and space, leaving its "green" smell at the end of my nose.

The Enemy "Within"?

Nicola and I (with our other university friends Nina and Joy), at different moments, traveled across Southeast Asia and Australia in 2000–2001. Doing the typical middle-class student thing of traveling halfway across the world to voyeur in cultural contexts different to our own as a personal and collective "awakening," exploring the g/local horizons that we read about as young people. For a short time, I lived and shared a room with Nicola in the trendy and alternative space of Newtown, a central suburb of Sydney. I worked at a bank in the south of Sydney, in Cronulla, where local media instructed White Australia men to take to the streets and beaches to take back their land from diasporic Lebanese youth who had dared to play football in these spaces. The politics of race and ethnicity at the intersections of imperial, postcolonial, Indigenous, and diasporic space was increasingly being amalgamated in my thoughts and through my lived experience—reinforcing, for me, a broader understanding of politics, everyday life, and social inequities and discrimination.

One morning, Nicola rushed into our bedroom, crying uncontrollably. Something terrible had happened. She urged me to get up and come into the living room. On the TV, one image after another showed two airplanes crashing into the Twin Towers (in the United States). People jumped out of windows, the flames raging behind them. I went to work. My Scottish-born Aussie manager told us British staff who were working at St. Georges Bank at the time that it was sad, but we needed to get on with our work. Welcome to corporate global economics. The neoliberal, capitalist, and military response from George W. Bush (and his British donkey, a.k.a. New Labour prime minister Tony Blair) was to secure our Western way of life or civilization: a "war on terror." The Islamophobic legacies of this moment continue to reverberate.

An End

As a diasporic and British-born citizen, I wonder what I could know of India, which is only ever, at best, a translocal image of a place I do not inhabit. A place that I have come to know from traveling across the country on a handful of occasions, remembering the homeless man recycling metal to build his makeshift house on the landing strip at Mumbai airport (recycling metal more efficiently than many first-world countries); the hijras who I saw at a local festival, whom my cousin told me on my first family trip to India (when six weeks felt like an amazing lifetime) would put me under their *gagros* (long skirts worn underneath saris) and take me away if they caught me looking at them. What lurked underneath their skirts frightened my six-year-old self. I now reflect on these memories to learn, question, and relearn from my lived experience. I also query the things I have read about: feminist projects in India on women's health and fertility rights, the rape of Indian women by police officers, and lower-caste street cleaners who disappear as day breaks so no one (meaning: higher-caste citizens) can see them (see Vergès 2021). These are the images and knowledge that frame my seeing; I am mindful that these rememberings and readings fuel my motivations to write about marginalized communities of Indian men and women but that such musings are neither definitive nor representative. There is more to learn, unlearn, and relearn still.

2

Walking with Friends and Family

By making visible the agencies of first-generation British Gujarati Indian women, this chapter contributes knowledge to the work of grappling with the g/local and pernicious politics of divide and rule. The findings emerge from a broader study about these women's walking pastimes and senses of "home" and belonging (see Ratna 2017d; Ratna 2019). Based on research conducted with five husband-and-wife couples—Ramji (my dad) and Kesar (my mum), Kanta and Premji, Radha and Lux, Jasu and Manji, and Amrat and Hirji—the project was about and for my family members and our respective familial friends. I have provided further detail about the methodological approach and method elsewhere (Ratna 2017d; Ratna 2019). In sum, the process included a research assistant (my dad) walking with each couple on a local route of their choice (twice), asking the participants to draw maps of one of their usual walking routes and marking anything they deemed relevant to them on the diagram, giving each couple disposable cameras to take photos of the spaces and places that they walked through and across, and using materials emerging from this field-work to explore further their walking practice and experiences as first-generation migrants through semistructured interviews with each individual participant.

In this chapter, I focus on the interview testimonies of the women participants to center and further unpick their engagements in walking as a popular leisure pastime. First, I explore their health rationalities for walking to counter discourses that frame South Asian women in and beyond the United Kingdom as physically weak. Second, I trouble spatial and feminist analyses of the private and public to make visible the agencies of the British Gujarati Indian women participants, thinking about their walking practice in relation to work. Third, I debate how the walking routes and routines of these first-generation older women (between sixty and seventy years old at the time of the study) also reveal broader insights into the contested nature of their citizenship and belonging in times of economic austerity and as transnational citizens living across diasporic space. Fourth, and finally, I argue that homing desires for these Gujarati Indian women walkers are a lived and ongoing project, altering and simultaneously renewing attachments to local spaces and places of "home" and belonging in the United Kingdom.

Through the different sections of this chapter, family and friends are positioned as providing a crucial network of support, enabling the Gujarati Indian women not only to survive during the initial phases of arriving in the United Kingdom but to thrive and create "roots" in their local spaces of home and belonging in northwest London. Moreover, it is the "news" that is shared while communing together—walking and talking, for instance—that enables the women walkers not only to "see" the world outside their windows (of the family house) but to share knowledge and powerful discourses with their family members and friends, to continually (re)position themselves as respectable, middle-class, Indian women citizens who belong in the United Kingdom (rather than any other ancestral locations outside of the United Kingdom). Walking, therefore, is an important conduit for them to travel (physically and metaphorically) across diasporic time and space. Before exploring these findings further, the decolonial significance of "doing" memory work, as a theoretical and methodological approach, is considered next.

In her evocative paper "The Scent of Memory," Avtar Brah (1999) writes about the death of a White English woman in a place called Southall (southwest of London). Brah paints a picture of a predominantly White local community in the 1980s, changing with the arrival of migrants from the colonies (including from the Indian subcontinent), which may have led to the White woman's growing sense of loss and melancholia. Brah's story travels through time and space, capturing a multicultural paradox (Back 1993, 1996)—that is, different racial and ethnic communities living side by side, enabling moments of friendship as well as racial antagonisms and conflict to emerge (see also Ratna 2019).

In another paper written by Nirmal Puwar (2012) about the Mandaap Community Centre in Southall—where Brah was a community support worker—Puwar writes about the life stories of South Asian women migrants who would have been arriving when the White woman in Brah's paper was mourning. It is my intention here not to provide a deeper analysis of these sociodemographic changes (see Ratna 2017d and chapter 3 for further context) but to pause here to think further about memory work, to recognize that there is another type of remembering at play in Puwar's analysis, which traces cultural continuities and flows of leisure (dancing and listening to music, to be specific) that give identity and pleasure to the South Asian migrants at the center of her paper. Recalling and reciting musical and dancing cultures, for example, in new and different ways expresses a "homing desire"— that is, celebrating the past to reimagine life in new times and in new places of home and belonging. These cultural pastimes are not necessarily about the dream of returning to an "original" home in South Asia (which probably no longer exists as communities, spaces, and places change); they are about finding meaningful ways to live *across* diaspora space (Brah 1996).

Arguably, this involves processes of cultural diffusion and syncretism and the emergence of new cultural traditions and leisure pastimes, including those of sport (see Ali, Kalra, and Sayyid 2006;

Burdsey, Thangaraj, and Dudrah 2013). I am especially in awe of how the filming process was used by Brah and her community worker peers to encourage those who attended the Mandaap Centre to capture their own life stories (see Puwar 2012). Even before filming was accepted as a novel and creative means to record leisure lives (Ratna 2017d), Indigenous and decolonial traditions from South Asia are remembered as an important way of knowing—that is, by sharing and retelling stories as a leisure pastime in and of itself (Puwar 2012). I specifically value such storytelling traditions, as I fondly recall sitting with my family members and friends in India and the United Kingdom to remember "our lives" outside of Western, White, and colonial constructions of "us" as racial and ethnic Others (see chapter 1).

Wishing to center oral storytelling traditions in my walking study, I found it was less easy to orchestrate as well as record sporadic moments, when the couples were walking and telling stories to one another, for the purposes of this study. I also found that when the women were sitting together chatting, what they discussed was not recorded by my father, the research assistant, because he was sitting with the other male participants (for further debate on this, see Ratna 2017d; Ratna 2019). As I had decided to use interviews with the walkers separately rather than as couples, I was pleased that this gave the women the opportunity to talk directly with me. It became clear that the women had much to say about their life histories, memories of "home," migration and settlement, and their evolving leisure choices, pleasures, and desires. By enabling their life stories to emerge through the interview process, I asked the women in the family homes, in a private space, to recreate an environment that "felt" like I was sitting with my grandmother or aunts listening to them tell me stories of the past for my personal pleasure (and leisure) and not just as a form of research.

Researching the lives of my parents (with my father as the research assistant) was, furthermore, a liberating process for me as a scholar who must exist in predominantly White spaces of academia. However, publishing articles from the study was challenging because while the ethics of the project were approved at a university level, this did not necessarily stop reviewers from critiquing the *un*ethical nature of the study. As noted by racial and minority ethnic scholars who write about similar people to themselves, questions of bias and subjectivity limit methodological approaches (and selected methods) to narrow and protect the sanctity of mainly White, Western, Eurocentric, androcentric, and secular sociological canons of thinking (Ali 2020). As Bhambra (2007) powerfully argues, these sociological canons are forms of knowledge production that are based on the racial, colonial, and imperial project of enlightenment and modernity that delegitimates (while reappropriating and claiming) other forms of knowledge production. Thus, the entrenched institutional logic of Western, Eurocentric, and White frames of knowledge production are, ultimately, already always skewed to favor codes of practice that reinforce and reproduce the superiority of such frames of knowing, dismissing, in the process, alternative forms of knowledge production. In this case, these forms of knowing include intergenerational knowledge and stories passed down through family and kinship networks that can be valuable to the researcher and the researched beyond the research process (e.g., see McGuire-Adams 2020a, 2020b).

The use of the Gujarati Indian language was also an important element of listening to and hearing the stories of the women participants in the "basha" (read: language) that best enabled them to express their memories, thoughts, and feelings. I am proud that I was able to use my "native" tongue as another means to decolonize how we know outside of the English language even though I had to translate the work to English to publish it. Embodied and linguistic idioms that transpire in the Gujarati Indian language are not always easy to decipher or translate. For both my father and me, as fluent speakers of the Gujarati Indian language, this too demanded a high degree of responsibility to ensure that we translated with care to avoid misrepresenting or even abusing intended meanings (for further debate, see Kim 2013). Performing research with and on family members is not straightforward, but I recognize it also gave me social, cultural, and symbolic capital to write about *mara manso* (read: my people) in an otherwise alienating and predominantly White academic space. With this privilege in mind, I now turn to the task of making visible the life stories and politics of these diasporic British Gujarati Indian women walkers.

Working Bodies, Not Just Walking Bodies

The medical profession often pathologies South Asian bodies as "in need" (see, e.g., Nazroo 1997 for a critique), deemed at risk of ill health from hereditary conditions, poor diet, and a lack of physical activity. Unsurprisingly, with a few exceptions, the notion of "fixing" the South Asian body is prevalent in such health literature (Ahmad and Bradby 2007). Walking is often highlighted as a worthwhile pastime—an antidote for South Asian people, helping them take responsibility as active citizens for their own health needs. All the women from the informal walking group—Amrat, Jasu, Kanta, Kesar, and Radha—reproduced such a health narrative to explain their own desire to walk. The emergence of this discourse was interesting, as it repositioned them as "active" and arguably valued citizens, taking responsibility for their own health and well-being rather than burdening an already overstretched national health care system in the United Kingdom (Mansfield and Rich 2013). While justifying themselves as "responsible" citizens, taking charge of their own health and well-being needs, it problematically consolidated colonial representations of "them" (as a South Asian group) as always and already "weak," perpetuating an individualistic approach that "blames" failures in health on people and not a poorly funded health care system, irrespective of racial and ethnic difference. Arguably, the British Gujarati Indian women included in this study possessed the middle-class privilege of having the leisure time to walk (they did not have to work in their older age). I am wary of overly celebrating their walking desires and pleasures, as meaningful as they are, as reaffirming their valued status as citizens of the United Kingdom, knowing that racial and class inequalities impact the health outcomes of many other South Asian communities and Black and ethnic minorities more broadly (Nazroo and Bécares 2021).

The prevalence of a White, Western, neoliberal healthism discourse also needs to be unpicked, as it erases the historical and contemporary relationships that many racial and ethnic communities, including those of South Asian heritage, have with forms of physical culture. For example, before migrating to the United Kingdom, walking as a form of transport in and around local villages in India as well as leisure; walking around local parks on days off from work (Tolia-Kelly 2004a) was a popular pastime. For women too, engagements in paid/unpaid work signal that gender divisions of labor within the familial home, across race and class differences, rendered invisible other types of physical embodiments. Thus, thinking through the politics of leisure to include links to family life *and* work also is instructive to better understanding South Asian women's health and well-being needs and desires (Brah 1983; Leseth 2014; Nazroo 1997; Qureshi 2016).

Kanta and Radha, for example, told stories in their respective interviews about how, as young girls living in Gujarat, they worked on building sites and undertook heavy-lifting manual labor. For instance, they lifted large stones and rocks from quarry sites onto trucks and mixed cement for their male counterparts. Their bodies and hands knew both paid and unpaid labor, as working at the building site did not exempt them from traditional gender hierarchies, which meant that irrespective of class and caste differences, women were generally required to cook, clean, and look after young children (Devika and Thampi 2011). Arguably, this division of labor resembled the histories and lived realities of working-class White European women during the Victorian era (Grewal 1996).

Jasu situates the case of British Gujarati Indian women more broadly, stating, "Yes, women have always worked. Our Kanbi women [the 'name' given to those from a particular ethnic, lower caste and class community] in India do a lot of building work; they help build houses." All the women walkers also worked in a range of labor-intensive factory jobs upon arriving in the United Kingdom. The following conversation with Kanta captures the socioeconomic need to work—that despite prevailing gender norms about South Asian diasporic women staying in the private spaces of the home and men entering the public spaces of labor and leisure, she had no other choice:

AARTI: What work did you use to do [in India]?

KANTA: Laborer at the building site.

AARTI: Isn't it different [than in the United Kingdom], women working at building sites?

KANTA: In India, all women do it. Especially in Kutch [Gujarat, India].

AARTI: So men and women both work at the building site in India? Did you like working at the building site?

KANTA: No, you don't like it, but there was no choice. You must work to feed yourself. . . . Then we [her and her mother] used to go to work at a concrete quarry.

AARTI: At a quarry?

KANTA: Yes. Pebbles, small stones, larger rocks—what we mixed with cement to lay floors. We used to work in a quarry located on a hill. Dig stones out from the earth and put them in the stone grater.

AARTI: So you worked hard when you were young?

KANTA: [I've] done hard work.

AARTI: What did you do for work here [in the United Kingdom]?

KANTA: I used to work in a laundry factory for five to six years.

AART: Do you remember that work?

KANTA: Yes, it was better [than the work I did in India] . . . but we worked long hours lifting, loading, and unloading, and using heavy machines. When you are looking for a job, you take what you can get.

As physicality is often defined and measured through engagement in sport and physical activity (e.g., see Shahzadi 2018), it is unsurprising that the notion of being physical in/at/through work is unreported. These incomplete statistics reproduce the notion that some women from Black and minority ethnic groups are especially vulnerable to the side effects of inactivity. Arguably, while higher class and caste South Asian women may have had time for leisure (understood here as physical games and activities) during the height of the British Empire and/or watching sports such as cricket, hockey, and volleyball (Mujumdar 1950), it is *their* frailty that is universalized and often taken for granted as representative of *all* South Asian women. Women of lower caste and class backgrounds have not had the luxury of being or feeling "weak." Indeed, rigorous, demanding, and unrelenting physical activity is normal for them, and a casual walk in the park for health and leisure just does not compare.

When I implore Jasu to explain how she managed to do all this, she cites generations of mothers teaching their daughters to cope and survive for the futures of their families. Such intergenerational sharing of knowledge between mothers and daughters is an area of analysis that is often taken for granted in scholarship about the health and well-being of South Asian women. Yet rather than making visible this type of physical and cultural power, patronizing health images and discourses prevail—that is, the portrayal of South Asian women as people who eat too many ghee-cooked curries and/or need saving from the oppressive forces of patriarchal family cultures. South Asian women (and men), irrespective of their caste- and class-based relationships to work and leisure, are thus (re)imagined as needing help—to help themselves, to become active and integrated citizens of the nation (Barker-Ruchti et al. 2013)—ironically, through intergenerational initiatives and also moving more at home and at work.

Public and Private Spaces of "Home"

For racial Others, Rose (1993) suggests that universal, White, Western, and secular feminist readings of "home" as a site of patriarchal oppression do not necessarily apply. "Home" for many racialized women also represents certain freedoms; it is a place to escape the racist scrutiny of the world outside their windows (Patel 1997). Tolia-Kelly (2004b) also evokes how memories of space and place captured through photographs and ornaments displayed in South Asian migrants' houses create a "home" away from "home." I also noticed similar images of different diasporic locations of "home" adorning the walls of my participants' houses, which could be interpreted as supporting the "home as a haven" narrative. As noted in much of the literature about first-generation South Asian migrants more generally, women began to access public spaces for work, rather than leisure, almost as soon as they arrived (Brah 1996). They were not able to enjoy the sanctities and securities of their "homes," nor were they able to enjoy middle-class White constructions of leisure. Walking to and from work constituted part of their daily ritual rather than a lifestyle/leisure choice. As identified by Scraton and Watson (1998) in their research about South Asian mothers and the postindustrial city, walking across and through some public spaces often induced fear of encountering racist attacks (see also Amin 2002; Phillips 2010). Listening to Jasu's testimony about her home in northwest London makes it clear: her "home" was not necessarily a haven, as at the time, she was living with a relative stranger, her newlywed husband. Therefore, in addition to financial reasons, she actively wanted to go to work (see also Bowes and Domokos 1993):

JASU: [My husband and I were] like strangers. From Nairobi, to get married in India, it was like strangers.

AARTI: So you must have been lonely when you came here?

JASU: Yes, everybody's life was like that.

AARTI: What did you do when you came here to pass the time?

JASU: Start work from day one. . . . Yes, didn't stay home at all. It was just like that. Every woman who came from India . . . everybody was like that. What would you learn at home? You will stay within four walls at home. You learn at work what is happening in the outside world. You meet people outside, they give you reports about what has happened in their house, in other people's houses, and so on. Family reports so you get to know what's happening in this world.

Her testimony highlights walking and working to get to know "the outside world" and one's place within it. Such "family reports" and stories are likely to have been shared with distant members of the family, across the diaspora, to maintain g/local ties and relationships. By suggesting that solace, for her, did not necessarily come from staying within the four walls of her familial "home," Jasu also emphases the ties she made with people at work—new friendships and relationships with those similarly located as diasporic South Asian subjects in a new place of "home." Perhaps searching for a wider meaning to her life and wanting to stay busy to cope as a newlywed, she highlights the porous and transnational boundaries among her personal life, home, work, and "the outside world." She desires to "learn" about this outside world as a form of personal mobility, survival, and pleasure (Ong 1999; Qureshi 2016). Arguably, for many of the British Gujarati Indian women walkers, work becomes a communing space, linking new and older diasporic relations and friends, and enabling them to share "family reports" (read: knowledge) to aid one another in *becoming* settled, financially earning, *British* citizens.

As further noted by both Kesar and Jasu, spending time with other South Asian women migrants at work was important to expanding their friendship networks:

AARTI: What work were you doing here [in the United Kingdom]?
KESAR: Sewing machinist. I got work within a couple of months of being here.
AARTI: Did you enjoy that job?
KESAR: Yes. The factory was big, lots of people were working [t]here, lots of friends were also working. So we used to talk.
AARTI: What did you talk about?
KESAR: What we did at home today, what food we made, who came to visit, all that type of normal talk.

JASU: Every woman who came from India, your *masi* [aunt], Ramumasi, and everybody worked.
AARTI: So women have always worked?

JASU: Yes, women have always worked. Our Kanbi women in India do lots of building work; they help build and paint houses. It is not in our Kanbi community [for women not to work]. Our society is completely different. . . . It's not like you people, living your life. Our life was so different—look after children, do cooking, keep husband happy, y'know? I think women get all this strength [from their life experience] and are strong.

Jasu describes how women of her generation had to acquire "all this strength" and be "strong"—a positionality, she suggests, that "you people" (meaning: people of my generation) would not understand. This is a narrative that largely remains invisible in postcolonial analyses of the "South Asian woman," which unfairly renders them as meek and passive objects. Jasu is also clear that her husband did not stop her from going to work. She explains, "It's not in our culture to do that. Uncle supported me going to work." She clarifies that this family decision was partly related to "having to work to survive." Jasu and many of the women she relates to in our interview, including members of my family, had to work for survival, coming from a relatively working-class and lower-caste Kanbi community in Kutch, Gujarat.

For Jasu, Amrat, Kanta, Kesar, and Radha, leaving the "home" to go to work may have facilitated their social connectedness, but it did not necessarily economically liberate them or indicate that they had the same social rights as other working-class White women. All the women walkers talked about fighting for better conditions at work (see Wilson 2006). Lux (Radha's husband), interestingly, speaks about a job he had in the 1980s that required him to support South Asian communities to get access to social services, health care, housing, and education. These important government-led changes were important to the walkers' individual and collective senses of job security, mobility, and belonging:

LUX: [South Asian women] did not know where to go for jobs. . . . They did not know about the Citizens Advice Bureau [CAB]. They used to go to people who they knew for help. . . . I was one of them who helped so many people. If they were abused at work and had nowhere to go with their complaint, they came to see me.

AARTI: You said abused, what do you mean?

LUX: [South] Asian ladies, they were complaining that they had to do more work than what others [White English women] were doing to earn the same money. They came home and complained to their husbands, but they [the husbands] did not bother, as they were too busy with work too. They did not know where to go for advice, like CAB. Instead, they go to a person, *who is [the] head of the community*, and they take advice from them (emphasis added).

AARTI: And did they manage to change their situations?

LUX: Yes, they managed in many places. Even in [the] 1960s, there were our elderly persons—about sixty, seventy years of age—who in London used to go and stand for their rights against the government, councils, you see so many photos. There is a book [in the local library he walks to every morning] about local protest[s], especially in the Harlesden area.

I want to be careful here not to endorse all of Lux's testimony about the role of self-appointed "community leaders," like himself, who helped many local South Asian communities and "ladies" in relation to their daily, work-related struggles. Such a re/presentation masks the agencies of the women themselves and their own roles in creating networks of friendship and support (see above) to challenge discriminatory workplace practices. Many older South Asian women—for example, Jayaben Desai, who led the Grunwick factory strike in northwest London—were far from meek and mild bystanders to state oppression and discrimination. Jayaben, like the British Gujarati Indian women included in this study, are representative of a generation of strident South Asian women who challenged the nation-state in terms of discriminatory immigration, work, health, and education policies while also addressing racism from within the workers' union (Sundari and Pearson 2018; Wilson 2006).

Upon retirement, walking for leisure and hanging out as a female group of Gujarati Indian friends was a desired choice representing a continuation of the solidarities developed in/through the public spaces of work. Thus, the leisure time practice of walking has always been about more than just a way of moving and staying fit; it represents a continued means of maintaining an important social network. It also became clear that the walking friendship group flourished, as it had a primary purpose other than friends meeting, walking, and hanging out—that is, going to the local shops to buy groceries (Ratna 2017d). This everyday routine, while mundane, creates the time and space for the women to commune together and for spontaneous conversations and/or discussions to arise relevant to maintaining diasporic connections and to organizing their lives as citizens of the United Kingdom. Capturing these conversations as part of their daily walks was important to understanding how they saw the places and spaces the women walkers traversed; it made audible how everyday bordering involves local people doing the work of the state—namely, to demarcate those who belong from those who do not (Yuval-Davis, Wemyss, and Cassidy 2018).

Some of the women—Amrat, Jasu, Kanta, and Radha—in their respective interviews, for instance, referred to walking past areas that had changed due to the immigration of "Eastern European migrants" such as Romanians, Kosovans, and Poles (see also Williamson 2016). They suggested that several shops had appeared on the local high street, reflecting the settling status of these new migrant communities (Radice 2016). Many of the women walkers, despite their own experiences of being Othered and facing forms of racism, arguably contributed to the demonization of other racial Others (Ratna 2014; Brah 1996; Thangaraj 2012). Jasu begins to build a picture of this complex process: "But they [state actors] must look at whether they [new migrants] are the *wrong* person. . . . So many people were calling people to this country in the wrong way—pretend marriages, wrong certificates, and so on. Many people were doing wrong, especially Muslims." It is interesting here how she reflects on the presence of "wrong" types of migrants by linking to both other South Asian *Muslim* communities as well as the more recent arrival of people from Eastern Europe.

To understand this juxtaposition, it is worth tracing the migratory experiences of many Gujarati Indian women as twice migrants. That is, leaving India as a lower-caste Kanbi community with prior experience of settlement in East Africa (and for some, prior to being expelled by Idi Amin from Uganda) provided crucial knowledge about how to set up local communities and organizations to build a "home" in the United Kingdom (Ramji 2006). Despite their lower-caste Kanbi heritage and sharing racial discrimination and lower socioeconomic class status with other ex-colonials in the "motherland" (Britain), such prior experience enabled them to adopt a "middling" position between the castigation of African Caribbean families as broken and criminally deviant and other, newer South Asian communities (such as Pakistani and Bangladeshi Muslims) who lacked such migratory knowledge and experience (see also Ratna 2014). From this middling position, many Gujarati Indian (specifically Hindu) communities were able to collectivize and respond to Thatcher's "working hard" neoliberal rhetoric of the 1980s (see interlude 2), enabling them to economically overcome their prior caste subordination (in India) and to eventually access and enjoy a more middle-class lifestyle (in the United Kingdom). It is important to point out that achieving economic mobility though does not mean insiderness within the national imaginary is guaranteed and/or that their former caste background is still not viewed as inferior. Thus, class, caste, gender, race, ethnicity, and religion are dynamics that structure the vicissitudes of national inclusion and exclusion, often in ways that breed hate and discrimination (Yuval-Davis, Wemyss, and Cassidy 2018). Even simple walks down the street, for leisure and pleasure, are not moments that are devoid of such manifestations. Amrat, for example, in her commentary about walking and the rise of Eastern European neighbors on her street, espouses the populist politics of the far right, such as the values of the United Kingdom Independence Party (UKIP). In her interview, she brings this racist (and sexist) political posturing to life: "If they [new migrant communities from Eastern Europe] come and work, get the job, that's not bad. But if they do nothing, especially the young—get lazy, stay only for benefits, and [have] families [, then that is wrong]. We got settled before having a family, a baby. We were thinking of the future when we came to this country. OK, [it] might be [that the] ladies are not working, looking after babies—that's fine, but men should work. That I object. People living on benefits, not working."

In this type of populist narrative, migrant women's relationships with the nation and work become lost, reducing women's roles to domesticity and spaces of the "home." This speech act also enables Amrat to reproduce a discourse of "us" versus "them" (see Gozdecka, Ercan, and Kmak 2014; Spivak 1991), ignoring the connections between men and women within and across "old" and "new" migrant community groupings. Moreover, both Amrat and Jasu reimagine and perpetuate notions of Gujarat Indianness as modern, progressive, and liberal compared to the sensibilities of other racialized Others (Wilson 2006). Amrat's speech act, more specifically, is impassioned but selective. She does not have children. She also dismisses, at this point in her story, the anxiety she felt as a British Gujarati Asian woman living in a predominantly White area (before the flight of her White English neighbors). Thus, family rhetoric is a powerful discursive tool to position and reposition the "right" type of racial and ethnic minority community (Yuval-Davis, Wemyss, and Cassidy 2018).

Jasu's point about the "wrong" migrant and some of what Amrat is alluding to relates to the breeding of racial discrimination as connected to ongoing economic insecurities. Although the women included in this study are very much middle-class consumers, they continue to imagine themselves as "the poor migrants" who first came to this country (see Ratna 2017d). Additionally, not all Gujarati Hindu migrants who came to England were "penniless" (see Brah 1996). Nevertheless, Jasu goes on to say, "People come to this country without money, no job, so how will they survive in this country? They need a house, [but] can't afford to buy one. Where will they find money?" Our interview continued:

AARTI: When *apna* [our] people came here, wasn't it the same?

JASU: There were lots of jobs; our people were working very hard at that time. They came penniless, so they knew they had to work hard to survive in this country. . . . Now people's mentality is completely different. Don't you think like that? . . . Also inflation has increased, [and] people don't have jobs. If people had jobs, then all this would not happen.

Radha, in her interview about walking past Romanian shops, adds, "More [Eastern] Europeans have arrived. Original people [meaning White British] are not living here anymore. Inflation has increased, and things are more expensive."

To make sense of what Amrat, Jasu, and Radha are collectively suggesting, it is important to state that the juxtaposition of racism and economic insecurities reflects much of what scholars such as Brah (1996) and Gilroy (2004) have written about, scapegoating the arrival of migrants for the failings of the state and the insidious erosion of the welfare system. What becomes apparent through the testimonies of these British Gujarati Indian women is that their ongoing ambivalences about belonging are reenacted through existing social and economic hierarchies, reproducing those unequal power arrangements in the process (Ratna 2019). Unsurprisingly, many of the middle-class Gujarati Indian women in this study are able to relocate themselves as a valued and settled community through the scapegoating of a myriad of racial and ethnic Others.

Translocal Lives

As long-term, settled migrants, many of the British Gujarati Indian women walkers had spent most of their adult lives in the United Kingdom. Thus, debates about their own migration status, settlement, and maintaining diasporic relations and connectivities were things they had previously considered. For example, common responses to the question "Where is home for you?" included the following:

AMRAT: My house is here; this is my home.

AARTI: Here?

AMRAT: My home, *natural* home, is here.

AARTI: Your *natural* home?

AMRAT: Yes, this is my home. [In] other places, I feel like I am on holiday. I don't like staying for a long time in India.

KESAR: We are living here [England] for a long time. So we like it here. We don't want to go anywhere else. We are used to [being] here, so we like it here.

JASU: I live here [England], but I still miss my country, so I go back every year.

While the women had contesting views about the nature and extent of their visits back home—to their local and ancestral places of home and belonging—a critical reading of their testimonies also reveals the impacts of the aging process and their health care needs (see also interlude 2). For example, in a conversation with Radha about her preference to stay in the United Kingdom, she suggests, "One problem is medical conditions. For [those] you have to stay here [in the United Kingdom]. If you get old, at least the children will meet you. I think it is all right here. . . . You are settled here, so this is your country. Even those who talk of going back will not go back."

Family and kinship ties across space and time increasingly bind her life to the United Kingdom. Interestingly, the ambiguity of Jasu's response to a follow-up question about where she sees her home is telling. Irrespective of her perceptions of where she locates home, her house in India or in the United Kingdom, she has the economic resources (and British passport) to *choose* how to split her time between both sites:

JASU: I feel like my house is there [in India] because I spent my childhood over there. I still think that is my house. I have never thought this [the United Kingdom] is my home country. . . . The population has increased, and the *gham* [village] is no longer a gham but a city. . . . It's not the gham anymore, but I still want to go there. I will come back to the U.K. every two to three years.

AARTI: So you will not stay there permanently?

JASU: Permanently? I don't think so. To never come back to the U.K. is not on my mind.

AARTI [*TEASINGLY*]: You have a nice holiday house [in the United Kingdom]. So who will do your allotment?

JASU: Jayesh, he will do it. . . . If I miss my children, then I will come back, I have a choice.

AARTI: Why do you have a choice?

JASU: I have money. Have worked all my life, very hard. Have saved money, *so can do what I like.*

The economic capital Jasu refers to gives her choice as an aging yet flexible British citizen—the ability to decide her future (see also Ong 1999) as an act of empowerment and entitlement that working, as a first-generation migrant, has given her.

In relation to discussions about other translocal sites and spaces (see Ratna 2017d for further debate), it became evident that many of the walkers returned to their ancestral places of "home" on an annual basis—usually at the same time of year, when it was winter in the United Kingdom and summer in India—for holidays that could last from several weeks, to six months, to even a year. During their leisurely sojourns in India, many of the same group of friends would walk together daily, congregating at local places to pass the time and chat (see also Ratna 2017d). The women describe this time as follows:

AMRAT: Go to sister's house, go to eat at father-in-law's house, go to walk every day in the evening. After dinner, we leave [the] house at 5:00, and then we go for a walk. Meet friends, wait for some, get together, and talk. Sitting at Lake Kari Mori [in the village of Madhapur]. Sit for a while and then walk home again.

AARTI: Do you go walking over there?

KANTA: Yes, *we all* go walking there also (emphasis added).

AARTI: Where do you go walking?

KANTA: There is a park in the village; we go there and take a few rounds and then sit and then come back home.

When I probed who Amrat met up with, it became clear that many British Asian expats often meet up during return trips (Ramji 2006) rather than walk with those Indians who are local to the village:

AMRAT: Local women don't have time [for leisure]. They don't like this. We all walk, talk, and come back home. We have general talks about home in the U.K., cooking, shopping, clothes, sometimes about films—depends on personal interest. We all hear them.

AARTI: So you are a lot of women or one or two?

AMRAT: Ten to fifteen.

AARTI: Really? Then you all come back to the U.K.?

AMRAT: Yes, some stay for six months, some for four months, some for two months. Those who work [in the United Kingdom] stay for four to five weeks.

Both Amrat and Kanta suggest that the social networks they have in India are not old, familial ties that link them to a past time when they previously lived there but connections with friends and family members from home, in the United Kingdom, who would be visiting the local gham at the same time as them—arguably, reinforcing their relationships to one another, as *British* citizens and friends, while spending their holiday/leisure time together in India (see also Ramji 2006).

The friendship and walking group is a closed communing site, not necessarily open to local people who do not share a preference for walking as a form of leisure and/or who do not have the time outside of work commitments. The exclusive nature of this site also reveals that while it was important to claiming rights to public spaces of work and leisure when the women were new migrants to the United Kingdom, increasingly, the group shares stories and knowledge relevant to retaining their middle-class interests (and leisure time preferences), which do not necessarily resonate with the class and caste circumstances of local South Asian villagers. Thus, the utility of walking for galvanizing a broader grouping or community of actors across social differences is limited.

Conclusion

A study about the walking pastimes of my parents and their friends, all first-generation Gujarati Indian migrants, created various challenges. Anticipating and responding to the challenges posed by this study not only enabled me to make visible complex, gendered power relationships; it worked against the colonial, Western, Eurocentric, secular, and ethnocentric grain of how we do research, for who, and for what purpose. The politics of the Gujarati Indian women walkers also provided a much-needed counterpoint to studies that are mostly male focused and based on male theorizing. The walking practices of first-generation Gujarati Indian women reveal their historical, diasporic, and dynamic senses of self. These are framed and understood by them in relation to class, caste, ethnic, and religious subjectivities as well as in relation to a myriad grouping of other racialized Others. Arguably, focusing on walking as a leisure pastime raised unexpected but politically important questions about changing, contradictory, ambivalent, and contested constructions of home and belonging.

One of the most significant aspects of this study was acknowledging how changing familial dynamics within the United Kingdom kept the walkers rooted in the United Kingdom, on the one hand, while their traveling cultural engagements in walking with friends from the United Kingdom in India reinforced and further cemented "home," as in the United Kingdom, on the other hand. Importantly, the walking and talking culture enacted between the women is conducive to creating a shared space of "commons" that is as unifying as it is exclusionary—that is, excluding other South Asian women (across citizenship, class, and caste ties) and other ethnic and racial minority groups. Yet the ability to listen to and hear stories shared while walking and talking across space and time adds to the confidence that these *British* Asian Gujarati women express about their senses of home and belonging as firmly rooted in the United Kingdom rather than any other South Asian diasporic site.

INTERLUDE TWO:
HOMING DESIRES

Interweaving personal memories, empirical material emerging from my walking study (see chapter 2), and more recent interactions with members of the walking group, I consider "home" as an evolving project of belonging. The pieces of prose that feature in this interlude are my stories; they unpick what frames my "seeing." Moreover, they are used to alert the reader to the intricacies of how race, gender, and class are imbued in family and friendship relationships. They re/present a more personal and different way of drawing out the politics of home and belonging that suture the various chapters of this book. Four sections make up this interlude: re-viewing home as an intimate space for knowing "truths" about the world and everyday life, exploring "homing" as a socialist and familial project of negotiating a long-term settlement, reflecting empirically on the desire to return to an ancestral "home" and the significance of health care, and finally, telling the stories that are not told within a familial context relating to shame and mental health.

"Our" House and Other "Truths"

I remember a few things from my childhood growing up in northwest London. Our house ("in the middle of our street," as the Madness song goes) was home to three families: my family (who owned the house and resided downstairs), Rekha's family (who had a double bedroom and box room upstairs), and Janki and her husband (who had the second double bedroom upstairs). Like many first-generation migrants, sharing households with other families was common. Living closely alongside other families had both positive and negative repercussions. Friendships with other children living at the house (one of whom is still a friend, Rekha) blossomed. Sleeping on a makeshift bed on our living room floor, my sister and I heard many conversations not for our ears: when Kaka (read: uncle) got beaten up by the police (he was too "dark" in skin color to not be seen as Black) and when Rekha's dad, Ronnie, hit her mum. Many years later, we learned Ronnie had been imprisoned for raping Rekha (his then teenage daughter). I wish I did not know or remember these things—they lurk in the back of my mind, the stories of South Asian families, those of the men and women in my life at the time, marked by both domestic violence and police brutality (Wilson 2006). Even though I did not suffer physical pain like Rekha or Kaka did, I metaphorically feel it even now.

My mother took on her boss, the caretaker at the primary school where she was a cleaner. At my primary school, in fact—where she cleaned the toilets—is also where I was first racially attacked (beaten up by two older White girls). More violence. My mum with her South Asian women coworkers, through their trade union, won their unfair discrimination case. Chapter 2 is for my mum and for South Asian mothers more broadly, whose activisms taught us second-generation kids how to fight back when the line had been crossed at home, at school, and at work. These different racial, economic, and sexual violences are not just a South Asian "thing"; they continue to be common occurrences across the lives and circumstances of many other racial and ethnic groupings. Such intergenerational knowledge is built into my erotic and resurfaces now to help me make sense of the complexities of race, gender, class, and caste struggles.

It's a Family Affair

At the time of arrival for many Gujarati Indians in the 1960s and 1970s, including those in my walking study, networks of family and friends enabled them to become settled citizens (Ramji 2006). They provided much-needed social support and a money-saving system that enabled families to set up new households in a new country, with tenants eventually setting up their own households with their own tenants. Lux, prior to talking about his everyday walking practice, reflects on this collective rather than individual form of economic solidarity: "I had a house in Oldham, which I sold for £16,000 and bought this house for £51,000. At that time, [a] £30,000 mortgage was quite hard to pay. Some of us were only earning £80 a week. But [South] Asians had a joint family system: if children were grown up, they used to help toward the bills and other things. They stayed together. They would buy another house, again helping each other; it was a family affair. That's how we got settled."

Family support provided many Gujarati Indians—like Lux, who was an educated professional in Kenya (teacher) before his arrival to the United Kingdom—the opportunity to (re)garner the social, cultural, and economic capital to (re)mobilize a middle-class status. I would argue that in addition to this, many of these Gujarati Indian walkers were also able to foster their growing "middling" positionings in England (see chapter 2) because they worked together as flexible citizens (Ong 1999). Reflecting on the walking study, as I write now (June 2022), I am reminded about the social pleasures of being with *upna* (read: our) people (and wider South Asian collectives of family and friends) to learn from my parents and their friends. Intergenerational knowledge regiving me the strength (and hope) to fight for social justice at work and through other sporting and leisure contexts.

Homing Desires and Health

At the time of writing this section of the chapter, the United Kingdom is in the second week of social distancing to prevent the spread of the coronavirus, taking more than one thousand lives to date (April 2, 2020). My parents are currently stranded in India, living at their second home in the village where they grew up. Airports have been closed by Indian authorities, and no one can enter or leave the country. Two sets of tickets reserved, still to be used. While both parents are seventy years of age, I have not necessarily thought of them as "old" until recently. My father is suffering from an unknown condition (that makes his hair fall out and nails and skin develop a strange texture). The nearest hospital is a two-day bus ride away. I have never wanted them home more than I do now, where the migrants who keep the National Health Service

(NHS) running (before, during, and probably after the virus) can ensure that these British citizens can access the health care that is unavailable to them in their gham (local village/town) in Gujarat, India. When the walkers, both men and women, talked about their relationship to spaces and places of "home," health care was a reason many regarded permanently returning to India as unlikely (see chapter 2).

The rural and urban divide is important to address here too. Despite the historical significance of this northwestern peripheral state as an important seafaring route to Africa and beyond, a geographical space highly valued during the British Raj that enabled large communities of Gujarati kinship groups to move to the motherland (i.e., the United Kingdom) in the 1970s and 1980s via East Africa, much of the northern territories are home to Indigenous Kanbis (lower-caste farmers). Following the 2001 earthquake in the city of Bhuj, which is the central hub for the twenty-four villages that constitute this Kanbi community, Narender Modi (the then state prime minister) invested large sums of money to modernize and rebuild (damaged) state infrastructure and provide for services such as hospitals. Yet despite the shiny new corridors of the hospital building in Bhuj, it is merely a satellite clinic where doctors from larger urban centers make weekly visits for routine out-patient checks. While the level of diagnostic care in India is highly valued (compared to the feeling that the British health care system is underresourced to provide similar levels of care), any patients requiring more intense care, medical intervention, or surgery must travel to urban hospital sites. For my parents and their friends, despite their economic wealth and middle-class networks, their peripheral geographic location limits their access to health care. As British citizens, they have a greater capacity to access health care locally in the United Kingdom without having to travel any great distance. Geography, in this case, can be a matter of life or death.

The significance of this point weighs on me, as if I have only just realized that they have been planning for old age (and death), and where they locate themselves will shape the options they have.

Manji, Jasu's husband, who was one of the walkers in the study, died at home in the United Kingdom while Jasu was at home in India. We (my sister and I) were informed by my parents that Jasu did not know Manji had already passed before she flew home—a secret kept to make the journey easier for her. The weight of one son down (Rajesh, who died tragically in Germany in his late twenties), now one husband passed too, on her shoulders to bear. I know she must now draw from the well of strength she articulated so powerfully in her interview with me (see chapter 2). Destined to stay put (again) in the United Kingdom, she must reimagine and renew her life again with her older son (his wife, and two granddaughters) during her older phase of life.

Shame, Shame, I Know Your Name

Having recently read the work of Lisa Tillmann (2015), I am struck by the conversations families have (e.g., above about their travel plans) and do not have (about mental and not just physical health). I am interested in the "condition" that shapes "how we get along" as parents, children, and siblings. In Matt's story (a gay man included in Tillmann's research), this "getting along" is not talking about the alcoholism that circumscribes familial gatherings. Indeed, Matt's gay relationships are in the background to other familial "baggage" that is "pushed into the closet" but, nonetheless, fails to be contained by any (real or metaphorical) closeting—the shame of being alcoholics within an upwardly mobile, middle-class, Italian Catholic diasporic community in the United States. While I am not suggesting that Matt's openness about his sexuality with his family is a sign of the times—evident of homonormativity and the pushing back of marriage laws (across many U.S. states)—I wonder about shame, especially as it may shape, similarly and differently, continuing patterns of familial relationships across racial, ethnic, and diasporic groups.

In my own familial encounters, I feel shame that as the second-generation daughter who has been given it all (based on the labor of my parents' generation and their ongoing frugal life choices as middle-class diasporic citizens), my current unemployment status (at the time of writing) is not "the dream." It is not what I really want (see interlude 1). I want the privilege and salary of being a full-time academic in higher education who has spent more than twenty years following "the dream." But the shame is not having been "out" of a job in higher education temporarily; the shame is not coping (mentally).

This feels like—to me, at least—a deep-down "dirty" secret; having a mental breakdown is the curse of women in our family. I know this cannot be true (and men in the family probably have mental health issues too), but I do not speak about this matter or unveil this gendered construction of shame. I carry shame and chastise myself (even now, writing these words). I must "think" myself out of shame (for the sake of my children). Be better. The health of my children in this world relies on it. I am also wary of other kinds of shame that lay often at the matriarchal "door" (to the family "image"). I use *shame* carefully—not *honor* or *izzat*, as these words are tinged in neocolonial, Western, White, European, and ethnocentric academic vocabularies that reduce "shame" to the problem of South Asian religious and cultural patriarchy. I want to link shame to politics, gender, class, racism, and the nation—to structural injustices. What are the shaming stories that others do not talk about, and what would this suggest about structural inequalities, if they did?

3

Gendering the Racial Production of Sporting Films

This chapter compares two sporting films: British female director Gurinder Chadha's 2001 film *Bend It like Beckham* (2BK) and Indian male director Vivek Agnotri's 2007 Bollywood film *Dhan Dhana Dhan Goal* (translated as "Get Set Goal"; 3DG). While the films were produced across two different filmic contexts, they similarly focused on the footballing (read: soccer) participation of second-generation British Asians, specifically from Southall, southwest London. The films are somewhat dated now, but the continuity of exclusionary forces in football (Burdsey 2011, 2021; Ratna 2010, 2017b)—and the filmic cultural industries (Saha 2018)—persist, warranting this critical attention.

The chapter does not aim to provide a review of each film or adopt a culturally relativistic dialogue about which film portrays a "better" (however that might be judged) reading of the multifarious, complex, and changing relationships between British Asians and football. Rather than reproduce colonial distinctions between Europe over here (as modern and superior) and the Indian subcontinent over there (as premodern and inferior; Grewal 1996), I instead make visible how postcolonial hierarchies relating to the complexities of race, gender, and nation are reproduced in and through the films. I also agree with Anamik Saha (2018) that we need to go beyond an analysis of cultural representations to consider how dominant discourses are produced in and through cultural industries, including the film and sporting industries. Using empirical, historical, and secondary sources of information about the films, I focus on the following three points: (1) the re/presentation of racism(s), (2) transnational solidarity and resistance, and (3) cultural patriarchy, gendered relations, and sexual intimacies. In this chapter, friendship and family are also unpicked as part of the challenge of exploring the complexities of race, gender, and nation, especially as they intersect with other social categories, including ethnicity and sexuality. Significantly, I seek to make visible the sporting identities and experiences of women of the South Asian diaspora in and through this cross-cultural comparison. Before exploring these key themes, sport as a traveling public culture is reconsidered (see the introduction).

Sport as a Traveling Public Culture

Like many postcolonial and transnational feminist scholars, I recognize that the movement of people with different social, political, and cultural ideologies in and between places is important to understanding how meanings "travel" across time and space and produce, reinforce, disrupt, and change predominant meanings about identities—those of ourselves and others (Brah 1996). The cultural production of 2BK and 3DG responds to different and connected social, cultural, political, and economic contexts as well as technologically advanced forms of global media, digital, and DVD production and distribution, operating in and across both the United Kingdom and South Asia. Increasingly, since the 1990s, Bollywood films have included re/presentations of South Asianness at "home" in the Indian subcontinent *and* across the diaspora. They also focused on transnational flows, the movement of people, and cultural hybridity (Ali, Kalra, and Sayyid 2006; Mankekar 1999; Sharma, Hutnyk, and Sharma 1996). In terms of the films examined in this chapter, the relationship between South Asianness and football is contextualized in relation to the United Kingdom. Specifically, in both 2BK and 3DG, the intergenerational and gendered sporting engagement of *British* Asian communities, in the first decade of the millennium, is g/locally made meaning-ful. The focus on football is a departure from the analysis of other sports popularly connected to the Indian subcontinent, such as cricket and hockey. Football has also become a sociopolitical and economically significant "public culture" and, as the national sport in England, provides a significant context that has traveled across geographical space and time to become a popular arena in which inclusionary and exclusionary forces—in supposedly postracist, postfeminist, and neoliberal times—can be deconstructed.

Reviewing Racisms

In both 2BK and 3DG, a British racist past is invoked through first-generation citizens' narratives about their engagements in sport as well as their fights against everyday and state-based insti-tutional racisms. The presence of racism as indicated in these films reflects broader racial tensions and hostilities in London and other parts of the nation in the 1970s—a situation familiar to many first-generation British Asians (see chapter 2). For instance, the mur-der of the fifteen-year-old boy Gurdip Singh Chaggar outside the Dominion Cinema in Southall sparked a "long hot summer" of protests (Brah 1999, 17). This moment led to many young Black and South Asian citizens taking to the streets to demonstrate against overt and covert forms of racism. They also responded to other killings, such as those of Altab Ali in Whitechapel, Kenneth Singh in Newham, and Ishaque Ali in Hackney (Sivanandan 2008).

Although racism is acknowledged in both films, it is con-structed in different ways. In Gurinder Chadha's 2BK, for example, racism is viewed as a historical past. Indeed, the ongoing conversa-tions between Jess, the female protagonist in the film, and her White male Irish coach, Joe, are arguably meant to symbolize an antiracist present wherein football is increasingly viewed as meritocratic. It is Jess's family that is portrayed as limiting her career, not Joe or the institutions of British football. In 2BK, women's football and the football industry more broadly are portrayed as welcoming, multicultural, and encouraging of Jess's desire to play the game.

In making this point, my intention is not to outrightly criticize Gurinder Chadha's direction and her exclusion of contemporary racisms from the film's storyline. This is because I acknowledge that while 2BK was independently funded (from an array of sources), pressures to achieve commercial success are not easy to negate (Saha 2018). Many racial and ethnic minority figures such as Chadha do not necessarily have the power to subvert and produce alternative cultural representations. Saha (2018) further provides a compelling narrative that explains why many racial and ethnic minorities are limited through the governmentalities of production, circulation, and promotion practices, which narrow and make impossible other cultural re/presentations. Chadha, in this context, may have a relatively privileged voice in British cinema, as she is known for "doing" diversity work through her past film production (e.g., *Bhaji on the Beach*), but her ongoing success relies on her meeting the status quo. That is, she must present "difference" without disrupting the hegemony and cultural superiority of Whiteness in film, football, and society at large (see Saha 2018).

In 2BK, as is evident across many televisual dramas about South Asian communities, accepting that the "joke is on us" is a valued British sensibility (Saha 2018), even if the cultural tropes being mocked are narrow and homogenizing in effect. Arguably, essentialized, comedic, and problematic representations of South Asian communities, in addition to mobilizing the global power of "Brand Beckham," propelled 2BK to Hollywood box office glory, masking in the process the ubiquity of everyday and institutional racisms in both the film and football industries (see Burdsey 2011, 2021; Ratna 2008; Saha 2018). Chadha pushes the boundaries of filmic content by referring to the presence of South Asians in Britain and noting elements of their cultural and religious sensibilities, but ultimately, she conforms to a "feel-good" capitalist recipe for success (Saha 2018). Her directorial choices, read in this context, unsurprisingly must adhere to the view of Britain as modern, progressive, and liberal rather than construct a complex and/or more varied representation of South Asian family life. This monolithic caricature of

South Asianness feeds into wider public imaginaries, which makes it difficult to tell other types of stories about the nation and predominant race relations. Thus, a view from elsewhere, unrestrained from the orthodoxies of the British film industry, may enable the lived dynamics and complexities of South Asian families to emerge in addition to presenting alternative readings of the politics of race, racism, and belonging.

The Bollywood film industry presents such a view. As a multi-billion-pound, capito-patriarchal, global phenomenon (Jha and Kurian 2018), Bollywood, after the end of socialism in India in 1991, further expanded and diversified (Dudrah 2006). The rise of cinema production houses such as UTV Motion Pictures, which commissioned 3DG, demonstrates the shift in Indian cinema. UTV aims to give intergenerational South Asians, both residents and nonresidents, a taste of Bollywood *masala* through songs, dance, and dramatic plots with a "modern" twist, including transnational storylines and making sexual intimacies more visible (Desai 2004; Takhar, Maclaran, and Stevens 2012). Arguably, while cultural patriarchy and stereotypical gender re/presentations are evident across both films (see below), racism in Britain is confronted in and through 3DG.

In 3DG, contrastingly, the nuances of racism past and present are central to the plot. In response to the team's individual and collective experiences of racism in and beyond football, Sunny (the male hero of the film) is reminded by his father to remember "who" he is, "Hindustani," acknowledging that Sunny will never be able to belong in the predominantly racist environment of professional football club culture in the United Kingdom. Personal and institutional racisms are also evident in 3DG—for instance, when Sunny, despite being nicknamed "Beckham" (after the world-renowned footballer), cannot get into his local league's starting eleven (made up of predominantly White men) even though he is the top goal scorer. This racial exclusion is significant to Sunny joining Southall United, a team imagined to be representative of the South Asian diaspora. As a space of racial "commons," his inclusion is never in doubt.

During the team's weekend trip to an English seaside town—for booze, fun, and sexual frolics—the male coach reveals how many first-generation British Asian players were attacked outside a local pub by a gang of neofascist thugs. This emotive memory is used by the coach to explain to Sunny why his dad, despite also being a talented football player in his youth, is antagonistic toward Sunny's elite career: he does not want his son to also experience racial hate. In this context, South Asian cultural norms and values are positioned as important sources of support among a coracial community of family, friends, and football-playing (male) peers that would not be possible in a White sporting commons.

Like in 3DG, Jess's father in 2BK also reflects on his experience of racism playing cricket in Southall, which is why he worries about Jess playing football. Yet in contrast to this racist history being viewed as a racial past that no longer exists, in 3DG, the contemporary manifestation of racism in football is viewed as a persisting "truth." In 3DG, the predominantly South Asian football team is valued because they confront the Whiteness of the league and those in charge of the local governing structures (Lusted 2009).

Diasporic Solidarities, Cultural Translations

In contradiction to the depictions of racism in 3DG, Western sports, culture, and professional football players are still nevertheless portrayed as possessing the "right" attitude that British Asian players and teams should aspire to, consolidating (perhaps unintentionally) White supremacist and postcolonial hierarchies of power and control. To illustrate, in 3DG, the coach of Southall United takes the team to the Manchester United football ground, the Theatre of Dreams, to recall the past greats, including the Busby Babes and other world-renowned footballers who play in the English Premier League in more contemporary times. While these icons are adopted as symbols of British football prestige, it should be noted that these real-life players reflect a cosmopolitan and racial mix of global talent (Carrington 2012); economic migrants are given citizenship, to various extents, while the same is refused to other migrants who also have legitimate claims to citizenship (Jones et al. 2017). This visit is portrayed as a form of character rehabilitation, making a team of disciplined men from a group of British Asian footballers who are initially infantilized in their representation. Agnotri in 3DG, therefore, unwittingly reproduces South Asian male inferiority in terms of not biology but ethnic and cultural characteristics. They are lacking the leadership and determination required to make it to elite levels of the professional game (see Burdsey 2006).

The trip serves its function of bonding the team, inspiring courage, character, and a hunger to be successful. Yet this aspect of 3DG is contradictory, as it undermines the sense of community pride that fueled the rise of the team in the first place. In other parts of the film, for instance, the significance of the club as a familial and friendly "community" space—representative of the "Hindustani" diaspora—is re/produced (see above). These instances recall an Indian history and sense of South Asian diaspora, which unites Pakistani, Bangladeshi, and Indian players in England—albeit as part of a Hindustani nation. Ironically, this selective re/presentation erases historical and contemporary national, religious, class, and caste antagonisms. It is likely that 3DG, like other Bollywood films, perpetuates the nationalist Hindutva sentiments of many Indian/Hindu middle-class film producers and audiences and their affinities toward the right-wing nationalist Bharata Janata Party (BJP). As Datta (2000) notes, rural life and class struggles are marginalized in Bollywood filmic re/presentations and/or limited to films produced by regional companies. Thus, the individual consumptive lifestyle choices and cultural tastes of (elite) South Asian communities and the construction of India as a global, economically developing *Hindustani* modern nation-state are reinforced. This imaginary version of India recalls a time before the partition and Pakistani independence, when Indian, Sikh, Muslim, and Christian people lived together as neighbors, friends, sporting peers, and citizens of the nation. At the end of 3DG, South Asian diasporic solidarity is not only cherished but viewed as a significant means to overcome entrenched racist hegemonies in and beyond football (see chapter 4 for further debate). Southall United not only win the league; their £3 million prize money is used to buy their ground—as a symbol of their community pride—as well as support the financial status of many of the working-class members of the team (some of whom are depicted as struggling with paying bills and the everyday costs of living).

In contrast to the view of sport as a South Asian common and space to collectivize as South Asian family and friends to resist racism, the portrayal of Jess in 2BK reproduces a neoliberal story of individual talent—that is, fighting against her own family and the wider community to play the game she loves. Some postfeminist analyses may eulogize Jess's success as an example of "girl power," personified by the 1990s pop band the Spice Girls (see interlude 1). While racism, sexism, and homophobia are recognized in 2BK, Jess's ability to transcend such issues solidifies postracist, postfeminist, and homonormative narratives about both football and the British nation as increasingly inclusive spaces (Abdel-Shehid and Kalman-Lamb 2015). Her assimilation into football compared to the fate of her sister Pinky, who gets married in the film, can also be argued to reflect a form of transcendence (Abdel-Shehid and Kalman-Lamb 2015)—that is, releasing Jess to pursue her dreams at the supposed epicenter of modern Western liberalism: the United States, the land of hope and glory. Her story as a South Asian presents a "coming-of-age" story, but one in which Britishness and South Asianness arguably cannot coexist (Abdel-Shehid and Kalman-Lamb 2015). In contrast, in 3DG, individual socio-economic mobility is forfeited: Sunny's contract to play professional football for Millwall Football Club is given up in preference for joining a collective, familial, and South Asian diasporic sporting commons.

Agnotri, in 3DG, also captures the cultural hybridity of being British and South Asian, with different class subjectivities, in increasingly globalized and millennial times. For example, the polymorphous lifestyle choices of the men and women depicted in the film; the characters speaking Hindi and English and a fusion of the two, "Hinglish"; and the older and younger generations of men and women (of differing faiths and levels of religiosity) at the pub drinking alcohol, playing pool, and watching football as well as going to the "dogs" (dog racing track) and singing and dancing along to various popular Western and South Asian songs evidences the hybridity of this group of *Br-Asian*[1] characters (Ali, Kalra, and Sayyid 2006; Hall 1996). Indeed, the fashion, style, music, and street scenes offer the cosmopolitan "feel" of everyday life in Southall. In contrast, in 2BK, sounds of Southall are heard from within the private spaces of the family and community center, which further demarcates this urban locality as a traditional space compared to the supposedly liberating and modern space of women's football (and the dance club space in Germany). While only done for comedic effect, 2BK re/produces popular, political, and media stereotypes about South Asians as leading parallel lives (Phillips 2006). This dominant viewpoint unfortunately misses the opportunity to position a counternarrative that makes visible multicultural conviviality, hybridity, and friendship, and not just family relationships, as forms of community empowerment and resistance (Gilroy 2004).

The Question of Gender

While exploring ongoing forms of racism in football and British society, Agnotri unquestioningly portrays women as subordinated and/or as sex objects. Indeed, the female South Asian physiotherapist of the team in 3DG, Priya, is objectified in the film as Sunny's "love interest." As a racial and ethnic minority character, let alone a woman in such a role, in a predominantly White and male environment, her occupational status is rare. Yet despite her professional esteem, the filmic representations of women, both South Asian and White, reduce their roles to ultimately being either chaste or not chaste, Hindustani or too Western (meaning: sexually loose). They are also portrayed as women servicing men's needs rather than as players or professionals involved in the game as part of their own career aspirations, pleasures, and desires (Grewal 1996; Thangaraj 2015).

It also would be a fallacy to suggest that representations of South Asian women's sexualities in both films reflect modernizing and/or new South Asian sensibilities, as complex sexual relations have always been part of South Asian cultural history and cinema scenes (Jha and Kurian 2018; Desai 2004). Postindependence, the modernizing position of the Indian nation-state, for instance, was increasingly gendered and symbolized by South Asian women's positions as reproducers of the nation and as the moral guardians of family virtue (Mankekar 1999). In 2BK, while Jess is sexualized—presented as an exotic vision when dressed up on a night out with her teammates in Germany—in 3DG, contrastingly, Priya is presented as having sexual desires but, ultimately, is viewed as the voice of piousness and reason (see chapter 1). Indeed, her condemnation of Sunny's choice to join Millwall FC and his vacuous consumption of "fast cars, fast women, and posh houses" brings him back to the Hindustani family/community (see above), thus restoring Sunny's Hindustani identity and repairing his relationship to his father.

Sunny's character, moreover, is relatable across different transnational and cultural contexts, signifying a male "stud" with an impressive body, footballing talent, and cockiness. Sunny's "laddish" character (see Burdsey 2004) is "softened" as 3DG unfolds, and his tears do make him not effeminate but an "ideal" man. Thus, his hegemonic masculinity and ability to win Priya's affection are never in doubt. The success of football and British Asians' engagement with it more broadly as a part of everyday culture—watching football at the pub, betting, going to local league games, and so on—are recognized in 3DG. Arguably, despite the infantilization of South Asian men, as mentioned earlier, their bodies and styles of play contrast colonial representations of "them" as effeminate and not interested in sport (Burdsey 2006).

While the White supremacist, racist, and gendered context of football in the United Kingdom (see chapter 4 for further debate) is central to the storyline of 3DG, in 2BK, the women's game is highlighted. Chadha makes visible the intersections of race, gender, and sexuality, dispelling colonial myths about South

Asian women's fragility, physical weakness, and sporting ineptitude (Burdsey, Thangaraj, and Dudrah 2013; Caudwell 2009; Ratna 2011). Indeed, through transgressive moments in 2BK, the experiences of Jess and her football friend Jules in relation to their femininities, their irrational mothers, and heterosexuality are similar despite the players being narrated as two culturally different characters. That is, one grew up in a liberated White English household (Jules); the other in an oppressive one (Jess). 2BK challenges the notion that women and girls cannot play football, although gender is surveyed, performed, and regulated by players and their respective families—for example, based on the "fear of the lesbian bogeywoman" (Krane 1996). Indeed, Jess's heterosexuality is confirmed by her relationship with Joe, her coach. In 3DG, women's subjectivities are reduced to their gendered and overtly sexual bodies—for example, as seminaked South Asian women with heaving bosoms dancing in the pub and seminaked White women frolicking on the beach. Women are also present in/through other service roles—for example, wives/mothers, cooks, housewives, and as previously noted, a female physiotherapist. A White female in 3DG who represents an authority figure (for the local council) wants to end Southall United's lease agreement to their home ground to use this space to build a multipurpose, profit-motivated, Americanized shopping mall complex. Like the tactics used by the colonial male and female masters of the empire, she uses her South Asian minions who aspire to British(er) identities and tastes (see chapter 1), to halt Southall United's progression through the lower ranks of football competitions in England (see Grewal 1996; Spivak 1988). Those who desire to save the ground do so because it is not only the home ground of Southall United but also a space of belonging that is imagined as representing South Asianness (see also chapter 4).

Heterosexual Only?

While queer identities and desires are often rendered invisible in sport to reproduce popular and marketable images of *heterosexual* womanhood, Whiteness is often the frame of reference through which queer dispositions are popularly understood (King 2008, 2009). In 2BK, the sexualities of women footballers are rendered invisible by the film's failure to even acknowledge the possibility that lesbian players can and do play the sport, and this normative frame is crucial to reading Jess's coming-of-age story as specifically hetero- rather than homosexual. That is, her sexual desire for Joe, the White male coach, firmly cements her heterosexuality *and* that of her women teammates. Through such re/presentational choices, Chadha misses the opportunity to queer women's football as well as South Asianness. Thus, the box office success of this British film is achieved because homosexual longings and intimacies are made invisible. The heterosexual and White male hero, Joe, who stands up to Jess's backward family, is likely to appeal to global audiences in the West. Arguably, Chadha, through this British commercial production, has less freedom to explore sexual possibilities as she did in *Bhaji on the Beach*, where she made visible cross-racial intimacies by working with a smaller/independent production house.

Coethnic and cross-racial desires are depicted in other cinema scenes in Britain and across the South Asian diaspora more widely. For example, in Deepa Mehta's film *Fire*, she demonstrates the intimacies and sociality that are fostered not in public spaces—including those of sport and leisure—but in the most sacred of familial spaces, the family home. At home, the wives of two brothers act on their sexual longings for each other (Desai 2004). Jha and Kurian (2018) argue that while sexual imagery has been long present in Bollywood films and such cinema scenes have been open to inciting queer rereadings and pleasure, in *Fire* and subsequent same-sex narratives—for example, *Chitranganda*, *Bombay Boys*, and *Love*—they have become increasingly produced for audiences' consumption. Such cultural productions are nevertheless dangerous; they make visible the longer history of queer politics in India before, during, and after colonial rule (Dave 2012). Furthermore, they suggest that same-sex intimacies are not imagined as being "out there" but "in here"—that is, in the home, where religious and cultural purity is thought to manifest and be maintained. Home and family are also central to the puritanical construction of how nations such as India can produce and re/present its postcolonial and global superiority, on a world stage, for wider audiences to see and know. Thus, it is unsurprising that in both 2BK and 3DG, love and sex can only ever be understood as heterosexual. Moreover, the private space of the South Asian home is viewed as a "straight" place, straightening queer desires, rather than a space for sexual discovery and pleasure (Grewal 1996; Thangaraj 2015).

This hiding is further achieved through the storyline about Jess's male South Asian friend Tony. He not only keeps his sexuality from his family when at home but suggests to Jess that through the pretense of marriage, they can create a liberatory space for each of them to become who they want to be: Tony as gay and Jess as a professional football player. Arguably, in relation to the colonial context of effeminate South Asian manhood, Tony's presence is in stark contrast to that of the sexually active men in 3DG. Chadha's re/presentation of women's football in 2BK is understandable, though, as it follows a broader trend in the 1990s of emphasizing the heterosexuality of female football players (Harris 2005) in contrast to historical readings of *all* women players as lesbian (meaning: not real women and thus tantamount to being a man). In my own doctoral research at the time of the Women's World Cup in Japan in 2002, one study participant reflected on the broader culture that queried the gendered identities of women football players from the past—specifically, those who were perceived as being too masculine. Such players actively challenged images of women footballers as unfeminine—for example, the stereotype that girls who play football are butch lesbians (see also Ratna 2007, 2013).

Conclusion

The reception of both movies directed by members of a South Asian diaspora, but for different audiences, was mixed. 2BK, as a "feel-good" comedy, mocking South Asian communities through the reproduction of dominant cultural stereotypes, became a worldwide box office hit, even before including gross profits from DVD sales (Rings 2011). 3DG, about resistance to racism—albeit featuring the less popular Indian national pastime of football rather than cricket—received mixed reviews and only collected enough box office revenue to cover the production costs. It is hard to assert without empirical evidence why this may have been the case. Reviewers in the *Indian Times*, for example, snubbed the low-quality production and amateurish acting. Yet 3DG portrays many of the markers of hugely successful diasporic Bollywood films, which reproduce Hindutva sovereignty, modernity, elite middle-class wealth, community pride, and solidarity (Ransom 2014). In sum, however, the view from elsewhere (Connell 2013; Gupta and Ferguson 1992) is important to reframe how we see football cultures in the United Kingdom.

Both films and their respective directors are, nevertheless, caught in a conceptual trap. Colonial binaries are reproduced in post/colonial times, often symbolized through claims to modernity and morality and symbolic re/presentations of women. This is to suggest not that film directors—across various sites of production and across different genres—are unable to move beyond hegemonic representational stories, because they can and do, but that it is difficult to overcome hegemonic narratives and assemblages of race, gender, and the nation. To be clear, I am not suggesting that the directors lack vision but that they are limited by cultural production, packaging, and promotional strategies (Saha 2018) that serve the capito-patriarchal status quo. By deconstructing such filmic re/presentations, as I have done in this chapter, other stories also can be gleaned to make visible South Asian hybridity, family life, friendship, and the utility of sport as a site of both commons and resistance.

Note

1. *Br-Asian* is a term used by Ali et al. (2006) to specifically mark the increasing fusion between British and Asian sensibilities—in other words, recognizing identities as in a constant state of cultural translation.

INTERLUDE THREE:
THE HEARTNESS OF DARKNESS

The light—hallelujah—was promised to us diasporic Others. I'm going to share the "heartness of my darkness." Someone once told me that if I was about to say something offensive, I should give people a trigger warning. There you go, you've been warned. Leave, stay, but I will speak. This is my erotic.

Behind the desire to effect change in my scholarly work and to reimagine what this might look like in terms of theory, research, and personal praxis, I want to propose an alternative to coping. Not coping, just being (like my "mama" told me).

Not-coping
Coping, resilience, self-care, social networks, counseling, mentor-
    ing, anti-depressants, I've done it, and I am doing it.
I can't cope with racism, sexism, elitism, and the able-bodied
    environment I am in.
I can't stop seeing and feeling affected by social injustices and
    lived hurts, whether my own or that of the people
    around me.
I have decided
to not cope.
To speak out however it is received.
Audre taught me: we are not meant to survive.
I am not surviving, and being forced to maintain "professional
    appearances" is a silencing mechanism.
It adds insult to injury.
I may as well speak as I fall further down the crevices that mark
    these spaces.
I'm following the advice of a sister outsider who is different from
    me, Black, but her words resonate with other brothers and
    sisters.
Remember, we were not meant to survive . . .
I don't just want to survive.
I want something else.

Refusing the burden

I'm not going to apologize for being Brown and a woman.

I'd like academic institutions and those who are un/intentionally complicit to its structures and cultures to apologize to me, and to my sisters and brothers in struggle,

instead of blaming me for not coping, feeling unwell, not being able to snap back to the "happy face" of progress made, thanks for the words, Sara,

and to ask those who have privilege (in whichever way that might be) to acknowledge inequities,

to take the burden.

Please, I beg you, take the burden.

I can't take it and I don't want it anymore.

It's brought me nothing but heartache.

Take my heartache and raise me by one, put your career on the line to say the things that are unpalatable, not received well, which create discomfort, use your power to help those who are not you.

If you can't or won't risk your job—because let's face it, your privilege means you will survive—stop writing about racism, sexism, and other inequities, because your sweet words mean nothing without action.

I know some of you exist, I've met you.

You will take the burden. . . . won't you?

Accepting the stereotype

No person is an island; institutions and history are what we make them.

But we cannot do it alone, as that only feeds a neoliberal system that divides us rather than rewards us for putting the right thing above what's right for the institution. I don't have to speak or do anything to feel the forces of exclusion.

I think back to my younger self, who was nearly suspended from my undergraduate institution because I allegedly emailed expletives to my lecturers.

Do you think I did it?

There was no evidence to capture the anxiety that my body
    aroused in them.
My housemate queried, "What have you done?"
I wish I had been asked to leave; now I don't know where to go.
I've become the stereotype.
I'm so angry, and sad.
The superhuman act is too hard to keep enacting.
I've become the stereotype.
I need a White man to rescue this Brown woman, the other men
    are not White enough, or able-bodied enough, to fulfill the
    role of my rescuer.
There you have it.
My lived insight into the self-perpetuating hetero logic, of put-
    ting myself back into a historical, discursive, and metaphorical
    box.
I'll accept my fate.
But can you deal with my rage and neediness?
That's it, walk away, I'm not going to stop you.

To this end
I can't cope, I refuse the burden, and I accept the stereotype.
Does that make "you," those who are White—might be male,
    able-bodied, heterosexual, and middle class—happy?
If your answer is yes, well done to you, you won.
If your answer is no, what are you all going to do?
I will serve my master, so tell me, I am your humble and passive
    servant.
And, just to be polite, don't forget to go f-ck yourself.
You are f-cking f-cked, whatever.
Ironically, by embracing stigmas, both my upset tummy and
    mommy told me, you just got to get on with it; cope, woman,
    because that's what we do.

4

The Politics of Sporting Conviviality

In this chapter, I coin the term *sporting conviviality* in the tradition of cultural studies scholar Paul Gilroy and others who have appropriated the term by examining the leisure lives of young people (Nayak 2018; Back et al. 2002; Gilroy 2004; Neal et al. 2019). I privilege the notion of conviviality, as it recognizes the friendly potential of living alongside, or playing alongside, different racial and ethnic groups of people as part of our everyday realities (Gilroy 2004). This reciprocity is often ignored through predominant, mediated representations that favor sensationalist headlines concerning segregated communities rather than other kinds of lived realities (Vincent, Neal, and Iqbal 2019). Popular narratives tend to view these communities as "enemies" or culturally at odds with one another. As I argue in the preface to this monograph, sport has that convivial potential, those bonds made on the field of play, and many of us who have participated in team sports understand the development of long-lasting friendships (see interlude 1). Spaces of sport and leisure, therefore, often become viewed as more than ordinary yet part of everyday life. The comradery and team spirit that can be forged on and off the field of "play" are thus experienced as extraordinary, and this is what makes the experience "feel" special.

The symbolic value of sport and leisure has long been recognized by politicians and policymakers—for example, the use of sporting imagery to discuss the nation (e.g., see Carrington 1998). In the United Kingdom, the Policy Action Team 10 report also highlights the ability of sport and the arts to address social exclusion and community cohesion and to resolve social issues such as antisocial behavior and crime (Coalter 2013). This imagery of sport, though, can also be problematic when it is positioned as above politics or, more accurately, as an apolitical site of leisure and pleasure. Often, the mythical imagery of soldiers playing a simple game of football in no-man's-land during the First World War and calling an armistice on Christmas Day is evoked to show how sport can transcend the boundaries between warring nations (Adams 2015). Yet there is another analogy that is important to recognize: sport has been likened to "War Minus the Shooting" (Orwell 1945). Not only is sport positioned as a mirror of wider political and societal divisions; we must also recognize that conflict is embedded in how sport is understood as inherently involving a competition between two sides. As documented by a plethora of sport sociologists, institutional, cultural, and personal interactions that operate in and across sites of sport and leisure give rise to spectacular, new, and complex forms of discrimination—for example, the bloody massacre of the 1972 Israeli Olympic team at the Munich Games, the shooting of a Columbian goalkeeper for letting in a goal that led to the failure of his national team progressing to the knockout rounds of the World Cup in 2004, and the racial violence experienced on a weekly basis by young British Asian boys in Sunday league football in England (Burdsey 2004). Racism, more specifically, as others have reflected, operates in and through elite and recreational levels of football in new and persisting ways (e.g., Back, Crabbe, and Solomos 2001; Boykoff and Carrington 2019; Burdsey 2011, 2021; Carrington 2012; Kilvington 2013; Thangaraj et al. 2018; Saeed and Kilvington 2011).

The notion of conviviality is expressive of this paradox: sport and leisure as sites of both unity and division. Thus, my coining of *sporting conviviality* builds on the themes of this book about a racialized and gendered nation of friends and family. In this chapter, to explore sporting conviviality, I reanalyze material from my doctoral studies (some of which has been published) to examine the politics of race, gender, and nation through the context of English football based on the testimonies of nineteen British Asian (second- to third-generation) girls and women between the ages of fourteen and forty years. Respecting their wishes, I have named them as football "players" so that they are recognized in terms of their affinity for the game rather than in terms of their racial and ethnic identities (Ratna 2011). I focus this chapter specifically on four areas of debate: (1) post-9/11 politics of terror and international (nonmainstream) sporting cultures, particularly as they relate to the involvement of British Muslim women in futsal at the Women's Islamic Games, held in Iran every four years; (2) the convivial pleasures and politics of embodying a South Asian "rude gal" youth cultural style of resistance (and play); (3) the mobilization of agency and collective forms of power; and (4) the unifying and dissident practice of supporting the national and international men's football team from the perspectives of British Asian women players and fans. This analysis offers a critical commentary on the post/colonial legacies of nationalism, White supremacy, and hierarchies of race (between older and newer enemies of the nation). It also captures the racialized and gendered performativities of belonging to not only the football fraternity/family but also the British national family vis-à-vis continental Europe in recognition of living in an increasingly interconnected world (Giulianotti and Robertson 2009).

Playing Futsal at the Women's Islamic Games

The end of the Cold War (1989) did not necessarily end global struggles for ideological, political, military, and cultural supremacy in and between different nations. According to Fukuyama's (1992) *End of History* thesis, the ascendency of neoliberal social democracy presented the end of large-scale g/local conflict. Earlier historical cultural clashes were thought to reappear (Huntingdon 1996), including new and "extreme" reimaginings of Islam as a menace to Western values popularly espoused through the globally recognized slogan "war against terror"—for example, as detrimental to "our" (meaning: Western) way of life: freedom of speech and liberal democracy. Among the plethora of "extreme" media, political, and g/local responses to 9/11—in the United Kingdom and other Global North and South nations—fear of the "enemy within" (terrorists) replaced the fear of "Reds under the beds" (communists). The face of this newer enemy sported a beard, a prominent feature re/presented in satirical caricatures of Muslim men. However, the demonization of Muslim-looking men conflated all bearded South Asian men with potential terrorists, erasing in the process the g/local, cultural, and ethnic heterogeneity of Islamic thought and practice. Importantly, the lived religious practice of jihad is not a call for a "holy war" but a struggle within oneself for peace and salvation (Farooq 2011).

The aftermath of 9/11 continues to reverberate through g/local relations and international political and military interventions in parts of the Middle East and beyond (see interlude 1). While I by no means endorse the violent actions of militant dictatorships or rogue terrorist groups, arguably, colonial, imperial, political, military, and economic excursions in the Global South have often exploited Muslim-majority countries in the name of (Christian) "civilization." These historical encounters in Afghanistan, Iraq, Lebanon, and other Middle Eastern nations have long and bloody histories that rarely trigger similar levels of public vitriol. In relation to such Western provocation, the quest for peace and an end to terrorism (either Western and/or Islamic) has been played out across various sporting contexts—for instance, the plight of an unlikely group of Afghan men qualifying for the International Cricket World Cup (see Albone, Martens, and Knott 2010). Sporting projects have also been used to empower Muslim girls (Samie et al. 2015) and bridge the long and bloody divide separating Palestinian children from Israeli ones (Sugden 2010). I agree with Sugden, who reflects on his own involvement in Football 4 Peace projects in war-torn areas in and through the spaces between Israel and Palestine, that while social change cannot occur instantaneously just by playing football together, the experience of "playful" togetherness (see the preface) can create bonds of friendship that at that moment, allowing us to see (in loving perception) commonalities despite entrenched spatial, social, religious, and political differences that are inscribed in participants' everyday lives and realities.

As Chowdhury and Phillipose (2016) write, friendships (however temporal) can also include various levels of tension and dissidence. Arguably, these feelings lurk uncomfortably in the background of "on-the-surface" jovial cross-cultural exchanges. Not long after 9/11, at the time of starting my PhD, I read about a group of Muslim girls from my local neighborhood in northwest London. They were training to compete in the Women's Islamic Games later that year (June 2001). They were to represent the United Kingdom in the five-aside and indoor game of futsal. I recognized one of the players; we had both been members (although in different year groups) of our secondary school trampolining club. A friend of a friend gave me her number, and I interviewed her for my PhD study a couple of years later. However, her involvement did not mean that the other members of the squad—through a process of snowballing—wished to be involved in the study (although messages were passed on). In speaking with the male and Muslim gatekeeper of the team, the intensity of Islamophobia at that time made him reluctant to put me directly in touch with the girls for fear of biased and unfair reporting—they already had plenty of that. Eventually, with persistence and reassurance about my political sensibilities, some of the girls contacted me, and interviews were conducted with five of the players (face-to-face and one via email, as we were unable to meet due to geographic distance). Upon reflecting on this difficulty as a South Asian woman wishing to recruit other South Asian women, I have come to view this as indicative of deeper tensions that evidence that shared racial ties cannot always trump religious differences within South Asian communities (Ratna 2011). Considering the impact of the colonial legacies of the British Empire and the division of India, splitting previously connected Muslims and Hindu communities, a friendly encounter cannot be guaranteed *because* of a sense of shared South Asianness (see chapters 2 and 3). The postcolonial and intergenerational divisions between Hindu and Muslim South Asian populations are not so easily erased, even if those groups have grown up alongside each other and with shared investments in urban culture, fashion, and music. Friendship is also, therefore, conceptualized as a temporal dynamic and can involve un/spoken tensions *and* senses of togetherness.

In interviews with the Muslim women futsal players who had competed in Iran (in 2001), what emerged from their testimonies was an illuminating insight into the contradictions of sport as a site for identifying and overcoming social differences and to celebrate developing friendships as an imagined collective of Muslim women: *umma*. I was shocked to hear that despite the sentiment of "West is the best," the sporting facilities, technologies, and support offered to Muslim women in Iran far outweighed what the U.K. Muslim girls had ever experienced or had access to (Ratna 2010). Although England's women's football team has increasingly become a professionalized, sponsored, and institutionally supported outfit, much is still to be done to alter the view of women as second-rate athletes. Nevertheless, despite knowing this, I too was surprised that Muslim women outside of a Western arena had access to excellent sporting opportunities, consciously and/or subconsciously buying into the narrative that sport is antithetical to religious and cultural conservative Islamic dogmas and thus ignoring the possibility for other sporting stories to exist and to be known (Samie 2017). The re/presentation of Muslim (and South Asian) sporting women, voiced in their own terms, is therefore significant to retrieve other kinds of sporting knowledges.

The stories that follow had a profound effect on me—a reregistering of the circumstances of *British* Muslim women's lives in and beyond sport. Indeed, the captain of the U.K. team explained that if it had not been for 9/11 and the British government's desire to bring racial and ethnically segregated communities together to foster social cohesion (meaning: assimilation into so-called British "values"), then they would not have been given funding by the British embassy, which included paying for a qualified football coach (a White woman) to support their weekly training sessions. Player 7, the captain of the Muslim women's futsal team at the time, spoke about the motivations of the British embassy: "I mean, it was 2001, just after the Afghanistan bombing, so I think the Foreign Office got involved, as they wanted to show that we can build bridges between Britain, the Middle East, and Muslims all over England. I think they did this to show that the war wasn't about an attack on Islam or Muslims per se; it was about what was happening there."

This action was understood as a political gesture that in other circumstances may not have been supported (Ratna 2010). For these players, they were delighted that their involvement in the Women's Islamic Games gave them an opportunity to bring together their British *and* Muslim sensibilities, at the same time and place, while recognizing their wider outlier positions as Muslims in Britain. For example, Player 7 further comments, "As I have always considered myself as a British Muslim, the two kind of went together. . . . I'm British and I'm Muslim, and it was the first time I was able to represent both of those in the same place. . . . I'm kind of joking now that my fame was to tell everyone 'I played football for England' kind of thing, y'know? I mean, without the Muslim World Games for Women, I don't think I would have had that opportunity to say that."

Player 7's embracing of both her Britishness and Muslimness exposed other factions about her inclusion in a global imaginary of Muslim women. I do not think I will ever forget the story she then went on to tell me about the opening night of the Women's Islamic Games in 2001. She started her account with the following: "I remember the opening ceremony was just like the Olympic Games, but on a smaller scale, with fireworks. There was a display, all the teams walking out in this huge stadium, and everyone was invited, and it was fantastic—the feeling was so powerful, just walking with all these Muslim women from different parts of the world, and we're all united by the fact we're Muslim, and there for the Games, so that was fantastic." The friendly atmosphere was abruptly disturbed when they met up and talked with the team from Afghanistan. An Afghan woman asked the British captain, "Why is your country doing this to us?" The incident unfolded as the two women stood outside watching the fireworks.

They decided to move to a space inside so they could hear each other speak above the noise of the fireworks and the assembled crowd. "That's how the bombing sounds every single night. . . . You can't move away, there's nowhere to go to," the Afghan woman confessed. Player 7, humbled into silence, began to think about the auditory and embodied impact this sound could have had on her newly found friend. How to respond as the bearer of the British flag who, moments ago, proudly walked among her Muslim women sporting peers, representing one of the nations that were unleashing the bombs that were the source of her companion's distress? She could say nothing. She reflects, "I think we did a great job in terms of bridging some of the gaps between their players and our players, 'cause we have a common bond, y'know, we are all Muslim there together. . . . But how far that extends through the country is another thing."

She later elucidates that at home in the United Kingdom, the "gaps" that divide people are not so easily bridged. She goes on to tell a story about being at a local park playing football with her friends and cousins. A set of boys "came over and said we were Pakis" and shouted menacingly "We'll teach you how to play football!" before chasing after them. Player 7 attests, "We were set on by a group of seventeen-, eighteen-year-old White boys, and we were actually beaten up for playing football in the park." Despite growing up in England and her pride in representing *her* nation, everyday encounters circumscribed through the wider politics of division and religious hate meant that her presence was not wanted or valued by other White local community members. Thus, the power of football as a communing site cannot be taken for granted; it also divides and is a space where physical violence can manifest.

For many Muslim women, the hijab becomes synonymous with Otherness. Player 6, for example, talked about going to watch a football game at Anfield (Liverpool Football Club's home ground) and feeling the weight of the stares on her hijabi head. She felt relieved to have her brothers with her to "Brown out" the space together (Thangaraj 2012). She reflects, "Well, with Liverpool, it's not that bad, as there are quite a lot of British Asian supporters anyway. But . . . with the headscarf on, it's kind of weird. Nobody says anything or does anything, but sometimes you do *feel* it. . . . I've got to the stage where I'm not worried about what people are going to think if I've got a headscarf on; I just get on with it" (emphasis added). Being among her family gave her the strength to inhabit this White space, and as the game went on, attention shifted away from her hijab—and this Brown pocket of the stadium—to the game itself. She began to enjoy the atmosphere as the match progressed.

While inclusion may have limits for some of the Muslim women who I spoke to as players of the game post-9/11 (and 7/7), their fandom also captures both the pleasure and pain of being engaged in football subcultures. Although some everyday "gaps" and that *feeling* of difference seem difficult to transcend, this does not mean that "bridges" cannot be built or spaces cannot be occupied to "Brown out" and create new and more inclusive places of being and belonging (Bey 2019; Thangaraj 2015). Arguably, coming together as Brown women in and through spaces of football participation and fandom can hold other ontological possibilities for (re)claiming spaces as theirs and for them.

"Rude Gal inna Ingerland"

The cultural and global bricolage that shapes the lives of the British Asian women participants included in my doctoral study, as Western women living in an increasingly mediated society, is important to consider—in terms of not just lived expressions of identity and leisure lifestyles but also responses to g/local circumstances (see also chapter 3). My thoughts turn to Player 1, who was fourteen years old at the time I interviewed her. She was born in southwest London, puts attitude into her football performances, and is confident in her right to play the game (a predominantly White and middle-class women's sport). She reminds me of my niece (see the preface), as it is in comparison to my family members and friends that I first recognized Player 1 as akin to being a "rude gal," with her accent, the appropriation of Jamaican patois, and the creation of urban slang to respond to contemporary social trends and youth cultural pastimes.

While a generation apart, of different faith backgrounds, and from different parts of London, something about Player 1 felt familiar. She also could be a version of my former sixteen-year-old "self"—the one who unlearned being feisty and speaking in a familiar language with her friends and family to enter and be relatively accepted within the gated and hierarchical (White and middle-class) communities of academia. I evoke this former self more and more as a conscious choice, a survival strategy (Lorde [1984] 2007). Thinking about my own experience, I recognize Player 1's words, actions, and feisty attitude as parts of a strategy to stake a claim to a different environment: local amateur women's football. She states that she plays hard even if she might be small, suggesting that she does not want people (me, in this interview) to think she is not strong (because of her South Asian heritage). She loves tackling, and if someone gives her "grief" on the playing field (meaning: a hard time), she is not scared to play rough, but fair, in response. She says her teammates were surprised when she first joined a local amateur women's team, as she felt that it was not what they expected to see (see chapter 1). But her continued participation has led to some internal recognition on the team for her playing credentials. Shared experiences of physicality and physical pleasure are important to mark here not only because they refute stereotypical positionings of South Asian women as physically weak but also because they signal a corporeal context that *links* women across racial and ethnic differences—that is, the "physical" sinews that tie the players together and enable other types of connections on and off the field of play (see also Thangaraj 2015).

Similarly fierce attitudes and playing strengths also became evident during the time (six months) that I spent training with a predominantly British Asian girls' football team. They played tough and were not afraid of going to tackle hard for the ball or heading to beat their opponent in the air. For both Player 1 and the British Asian Football Club (BAFC) girls, turning up the ends of their baggy "joggers" (read: jogging pants) to show their ankles and folding over their waistbands to reveal the manufacturer's label—Nike, Adidas, Puma, and Converse—were aspects of their fashion and style. As conspicuous and savvy consumers, these fourteen- to fifteen-year-old girls (at the time I was with the team in 2004) were image conscious (see Ratna 2010). For example, they talked about borrowing clothes from older siblings and friends as a strategy to ensure that they looked "the part" when going to town on a shopping trip or meeting up with friends in their neighborhoods and/or at a local park. This familial and friendship network of support, sharing valuable cultural commodities as British Asian girls living in a particularly deprived area, was crucial to achieving this racial (and gendered) performativity of rude galness. They used their collective resources to be "who they wanted to be" (see interlude 1)—albeit as both a playful style *and* a form of resistance. As noted, "Browning out" spaces of sport and leisure is a way to claim "our" space (Thangaraj 2015). Alternatively, these spaces may be interpreted as a "commons" to share knowledge and resources significant to not only "playing" the rude gal but also embodying their citizenship when it is questioned or queried.

The policing of femininity was a crucial point of divergence for the girls at BAFC. Many of the girls on this team adapted their rude gal and feminine style with the use of accessories and makeup and how they did their hair. This included nuanced layers of re-creating a feminine look "with attitude." I think of Missy Elliott as a popular musical icon who embodied this fierce rude gal style in the predominantly male spaces of hip-hop, crafting a look that is feminine (and ensuring that she is read as a "woman") but without appearing as a "hoochie mama"—that is, the problematic image of Black women that only frames them in sexual terms. With the twenty-four-hour satellite access to channels such as MTV, the styles of cultural icons such as pop musicians Beyoncé and Rihanna, for example, were more significant for the girls at BAFC than, I would suggest, other women football players. At the time, Black role models included the England manager Hope

Powell (1998–2013) and the striker Rachel Yankey (1997–2013). This is to suggest not that these two players are not important to recognize in terms of their achievements but that they did not resonate with this group of young British Asian women as other popular cultural icons did.

Other members of BAFC found this gendered performance and energy a distraction from what they were really concerned about—that is, being good football players and not just *girls* playing the game. Yet the girls' friendship—despite their differing levels of rude galness—was nevertheless important to dealing with the racisms they experienced. For all of them, racism was not new. Since they had begun to play as a predominantly British Asian team in a mainly White local league, they had become used to racist name-calling. For many of these British Asian girls and women, this did not stop them from playing on a weekly basis, knowing they had "each other's backs." Popular slogans such as "We won't be knocked like that," "As long as we have each other," and "We fight them where it counts" were used by the players to suggest how they would deal with racism by confronting it where it mattered to them most: on the field of play.

Some of the other players I interviewed as part of the study expressed other kinds of views, including denial and reducing racisms to the acts of ignorant individuals (see Ratna 2007). Most of my participants played as the lone South Asian figure in a White women's football team (at various levels) and tended to lack the social, cultural, and economic capital to either negotiate a space of belonging and/or feel accepted as "one of the girls." One Catholic British Asian young woman, Player 2, did just this by using her cultural and economic heritage to become like "one of the [White] girls." As one of the many cultural styles representative of *British* Asianness, the performance of rude galness was a contested racial performance. For instance, Player 2 voiced her distaste for Asian rude gals, claiming they "speak a lingo that no one understands." When driving me back to the train station once my interview with her was completed, I noted the following about Player 2:

She jokes about the way *all* the British Asians living there speak the English language with a twang, funny accent. . . . In her jovial criticism of those British Asian males and females, she is at the same time distancing herself from them by suggesting she speaks "proper" English. In fact, she seemed to be placing herself in a superior position to them. This is revealed by the comments about her distaste for the area where she lives. She prefers socializing in predominantly "posh" areas. The rude bwoys and gals tend to go out locally, an area which she believes is "dirty looking" and where there is nothing to do.

Arguably, Player 2 saw the cultural performance of rude gal style as beneath her, reflecting class differences in taste and style as a middle-class (and Catholic) young British Asian person who, despite the sporting pastimes she has in common with Player 1 and BAFC, in terms of racial heritage, sees herself more closely connected to her White middle-class teammates (Thangaraj 2012, 2015). Sharing "commons" in and through sport is not straightforward, and class, race, ethnicity, geography, and processes of cultural translations and performance create complex alliances and points of divergence, showcasing that imagined senses of South Asianness can be fragmented, and spaces of commons can be experienced as both liberating and limiting.

Collective Resistance

The two elite women I interviewed for this study, Players 4 and 5, also embodied a fierceness and desire to prove to others (in this case, the antiracist organization Kick It Out [KIO] and their Sikh community male peers) that they could play football and "whip" the boys at their own game (word used by Player 4). Player 5 explained that she was fed up with being asked to attend awareness-raising antiracism events—campaigns that she felt, at the time, had done very little to highlight the women's game and the achievements of players like herself. She suggested the need to "kick out sexism from [KIO]," as antiracist projects could not be effective unless they accounted for multiple and interconnected forces of inequality and oppression. However, her criticism of the patriarchal control of the antiracist organization was also turned inward, speaking back to her own Sikh religious community. Player 4 and Player 5 joked about starting a team with Player 5's sister, who also played at an elite level, to win the annual football tournament held at a local gurdwara. Player 4 explains further, "Where I live, there are four gurdwaras. . . . All of them get together and do the 'Asian Games,' a five-a-side football tournament, and we found out that there was an announcement that no girls were allowed to watch. . . . I was like, 'Huh?' Considering that they knew about me as well and being Asian, it was just a bit upsetting, as this has come from my own community. . . . I thought they were gonna go beyond the girl-boy kind of thing." Referring to this conversation in her interview, Player 5 added, "The only way it would really work is that we've got to win the tournament. Then we can do a documentary. I think it would be a lovely story to get these women together that couldn't play at the gurdwara; they weren't taken seriously. We'll get our own little team together, and we'll go in and win!"

The solidarity and defiance expressed by Players 4 and 5 show how sites of sport, while hindered by ongoing forms of sexism and patriarchal control, provide spaces of "undercommons" (beneath the visible spaces and sites of the organizations) to commune— that is, to come together to share stories and plan actions to challenge issues therein (see the introduction). Both women were proud of their achievements, with Player 5 even suggesting that they should be documented or dramatized, perhaps like the film *Bend It like Beckham* (see chapter 3). What is clear from the testimonies of both players is that what unites them as women actors is their *shared* experiences of sexism across different and interconnected sites of sport and football; they "back up" each other (the phrase used by BAFC players). Similarly, as Muslim women playing football or watching the (men's) game, "Browning out" these sporting spaces enables them to cope with exclusionary forces (and feelings) as they arose. For the BAFC players, being together on and off the field of play was important to their efforts to challenge racism at local levels. However, their cooperative efforts were not without tensions (see below), as it would be naive to assume any space can be inclusive; power manifests in complex ways.

Supporting the Nation

In 1990, at the end of Margaret Thatcher's tenure as prime minister of the United Kingdom, the European project had been initiated to prevent the immigration of non-White commonwealth citizens to Britain to supposedly save "British" nationals (meaning: White people) from being "swamped" in *their* own spaces of home (Gilroy 2004). The Black and Brown outsider is now increasingly understood in relation to a different enemy: White people from Eastern European nation-states. As Lentin and Titley (2011) have debated so persuasively, the supposed failures of the multicultural project were replaced by political and popular rhetoric about the failures of the European project (which we are now witnessing through the aftermath of Brexit). This social history and context is not separate from the sporting arena but is a space where racial, gendered, and national histories are made and reinforced in the neoliberalizing cauldron of sport (Andrews and Silk 2012)—for example, the xenophobic reaction to the influx of "foreign" players in 1991 into the new commodity that would become the globally popular spectacle of the English Premier League (Wagg 2004). In 2002, Player 5 (with a fellow South Asian friend) went to France to watch the World Cup. The convivial fan encounter she recounted was informative, capturing a wider narrative about a national "family" and the significance of friendships while mutually sharing Western cultural tastes and lifestyles with other White English fans. I capture her testimony at some length here to demonstrate this viewpoint:

> I remember going to see Euro '96 with my brother and sister, and we went with my friend "Nina," so there were four of us that were Asian. We all had our faces painted (with the color of the British Union Jack); it didn't sink in for a minute that we were

Brown faces having our faces painted. It was the most normal thing in the world.

I remember walking into a pub in France, and I think it was full of those really yobbie [read: hooligan] West Ham types, Chelsea, and Millwall fans. I was the only woman and I was the only Asian, and everybody turned around, and they're the kind of people who would stab me on a Saturday afternoon in Millwall or something. But we were all there united for England, and I walked in and they looked at me and they didn't know what to do. All of a sudden, I just barged my way to the bar, and I was like, "Oi, c'mon, fatty, get me a pint," and they were just lovely. . . . They [England supporters] have a terrible reputation, but they just, I think, they just don't even think what they are doing half the time; they're just going along with the crowd, singing the same old songs. . . . I was standing on the tables and singing with them "Don't Surrender to the IRA" or whatever song they were singing—no idea what I was singing, doesn't mean anything, you just sing whatever they are singing—I must've looked really stupid. But they just completely took you in. You looked different at the beginning, but then they realize that you're just an England fan like they are.

Going to a public house—as a popular fan tradition—to watch, celebrate, and enjoy the match-day atmosphere is a common occurrence for many White male football fans (see also Kuppan 2022). Player 5 recalls how everybody turned to "look" at her when she went into the bar. It is a "look" that many racial Others understand as an objectifying gaze: What is *she* (a South Asian woman) doing in a (White man's) pub? The gendered context is crucial to her story, accounting for why she subsequently felt embraced by the "lads"—like she was "one of them" (meaning: an authentic England fan) and not an enemy of the nation. "Oi, c'mon, fatty," she said to the barman, "get me a pint." Her forthright statement, which may have hidden the doubt she felt about entering the pub, broke any tension that marked her arrival. The men in the bar recognized her willingness to drink beer, engage in jovial banter, and sing along with whatever song they were singing (Ratna 2014). Joining in and attenuating the political divisiveness of the actual chant she was singing enabled her inclusion into the English Barmy Army—denouncing, at the same time, a former enemy of the nation, the IRA. "Don't Surrender to the IRA" reflects a one-hundred-year history that marks the violent political and "Troubles" experienced in Northern Ireland. This sectarian divide is felt no more acutely than in the stadium on match days, when teams with Protestant links play teams with Catholic links in Scotland and/or other spaces outside of Ireland where international competitions and tournaments occur, such as the World Cup in France. This history is by no means small or insignificant; it is a threat inciting violence to retain or renege on a political alliance with England. For Player 5 to "dumb down" the English fans assembled at the bar by saying "They're just going along with the crowd, singing the same old songs" is to ignore the impact of such chants on peace and stability in Ireland at the time of the research, a situation that could erupt into violence, triggered by ill-informed judgments and misplaced acts of fandom. This is the complexity of belonging: the contradiction of reproducing racial, ethnic, and sectarian antagonisms to negotiate Whiteness and belonging in a nation-state where, in many other circumstances, "they're the kind of people who would stab me on a Saturday afternoon in Millwall or something" (see Player 7's testimony above).

The coach of BAFC also reflects on such anti-Muslim sentiments when he tells a story about how he and some of the older boys from the team went into a pub to watch an England game. The national team was playing against an Eastern European opponent, Macedonia. He began this recounting by setting the context: the game was being played in a predominantly British Asian region in the United Kingdom, and they had spent much of the day distributing antiracism leaflets (on behalf of a contact linked to KIO in exchange for match tickets). "Who do you support?" another England fan at the pub asked the British Asian men as they drank their beer. Despite wearing England tops, a symbol of their national pride and affiliation, this encounter demonstrates how race continues to be a salient feature of understanding national belonging. In contrast to Player 5's experience, this experience shows how racism can simmer in the pub. The players' masculinity (in post-9/11 times) perhaps read as "threatening" for this White English male fan and meant that lads who had gone to the pub for a social drink as friends were made to feel they did not, and could not, be part of the English national family. The pub was not a communing or welcoming site for them. Indeed, interestingly, their loyalty was further read as being for Macedonia—a predominantly Muslim nation—demonstrating another aspect of national exclusion despite sharing a White identity (see chapter 2). The displacement of blame from the state to racial Others was also a crucial factor in many "ordinary" people's decisions to vote for Brexit (even if their areas had no migrants from Eastern Europe living there).

The politics of hate and division that both encounters make audible cannot mask the genuine feeling of happiness that Player 5 claimed to feel among the England fans she met in the pub in France in contrast to the hostility the coach of BAFC encountered from other England fans in England—thus elucidating the gendered and cultural contradictions that mark the pleasure and pain of occupying a space of fandom across time and differing postcolonial European contexts.

Conclusion

In a more recent publication, I coined the phrase *hierarchical assemblages of citizenship* not to layer national exclusion and inclusion on a racialized scale from White to Black, as this dichotomizing analysis would have ignored the racial, ethnic, sectarian, gendered, and cultural assemblages that g/locally (and contradictorily, as discussed above) connect and divide communities through rhetoric about football fandom—who belongs to the national family and who does not. As outlined in the introduction, racial and familial imagery have often been intertwined and used to genetically map belonging across "blood ties." Even though the falsity of such racial science has been accepted, to various extents, cultural signifiers of difference (in terms of gender, race, ethnicity, and religion), for instance, continue to reflect broader cultural "clashes" between different groups.

Because of the complex, multifaceted, and g/locally contested asymmetries of power, the quest for social justice in and through sport is not a simple task. How can we address this contradictory complicity and reinforcement of anti-IRA sentiments, as well as Islamophobic ones, through the gendered and male-dominated context of men's football fandom, where inclusion/exclusion is contingent on historical and contemporary rivalries on and off the pitch? In relation to this, national debates about migration, race, and belonging become both increasingly toxic and mainstream. Thus, using sports such as football as a commons suggests that this vehicle for social change must negotiate complex hierarchical assemblages of power to achieve various social justice agendas, including tackling xenophobia, Islamophobia, racism, sexism, homophobia, and sectarianism. This is not to say that sport does not have a place and that it cannot be used as an instrument of change; rather, we must recognize the interconnection between sport and wider political, social, cultural, and economic contexts. Young women are chased in the park by older boys pulling off their hijabs, other women are drinking pints and feeling accepted, and yet other talented young girls cannot afford to do much but resist, at the same time reinforcing a capitalist economy where identities and cultural signifiers reinvent anew Black cultural fusions and styles of resistance (together and as a collective) to different forms of interconnected inequalities.

The rude gal in me—some twenty years later and no longer working class—wishes to tackle discrimination and foster inclusive changes to the women's game. Yet as the Eniola Aluko case demonstrates (see Ratna 2017a), institutional racism is rife at the highest levels of the game's governance. The academic "me" feels skeptical about achieving transformative social change. I want to end on a "positive" note, as books often do, including academic texts, but I can't write what I don't feel. At the time of writing this chapter (June 2020), with the ongoing deaths of Black men and women (see the introduction) because of racial injustices and police brutality, I do not feel positive. During this time, the legacies of Britain's colonial past and neocolonial and imperial present make it harder to challenge racism. Spaces of sporting commons, and the undercommons, forge inclusivity that, however temporarily, imbues a future still in the making when the alternative is frighteningly bleak.

Conclusion

South Asian Women, Mothers, Workers, Lovers, Players, Fans, and Friends

This book is an intellectual and personal project that brought together empirical chapters, cultural analyses, and personal interludes, switching writing styles to show different sides of my academic "self"—arguably, a "self" that reflects the emotional labor of making the private self public (Ratna 2018), open to critical judgments about my lived experience. As I suggested in the preface, I do not see this as just my responsibility. I call on scholars in and across studies of sport, leisure, popular culture (see Ratna 2018), and elsewhere to "see" what frames their seeing (van Ingen 2013) and what can be learned from this endeavor as a scholarly task. This is "my" erotic, and it is one that unabashedly speaks back to White supremacy and the heteropatriarchal and capitalist structures of both sport and higher education. It is not a neutral standpoint. I do not have the luxury to play the "professional" White Western scholar. Being the "professional" is damaging; it fails to do the work of transforming hierarchical systems of power and control. The writing I present in this book is more radical in ambition. I join my voice to the voices of other Black, Indigenous, and people of color in speaking to a different reality—our realities—of higher education and sport and leisure cultures.

Through the various sections of the book, I worked beyond Western, Eurocentric, ethnocentric, androcentric, and secular ways of thinking and doing research. Specifically, I recognize that writing "intersectionally"—through poetry, prose, and political statements that sometimes cannot be expressed in academic language alone—was a liberatory practice, knowing as I do that the "Master's tools will not dismantle the master's house." Moving beyond a more traditional style of structuring an academic and solo-authored book is not only a nod to the inspirational insights of many women of color writers who also use such writing techniques but also a reminder to people of color writing in the here and now: We do not need to command the oppressor's language (read: English). Even if we are the most eloquent speakers or writers, we can speak to ourselves and one another in terms of our choosing.

Moving beyond the "South Asian Woman"

Having spent the last twenty years writing about women of the South Asian diaspora and, more specifically, the politics, identities, and dreams of *British* Asian girls and women (of Indian heritage), I wanted to develop an analytical model inspired by a range of Black, postcolonial, Chicana, Indigenous, transnational, and queer of color feminist writers to include re/presentations that moved beyond fixed and universalizing re/presentations of the "South Asian woman." In this way, I was pleased to be able to tell stories about British Asian women more specifically as mothers (indeed, my mother), workers, lovers, wives, football players, fans of sport, and family members and friends. This polymorphous representation of their stories from these different identity vantage points expresses a more capacious understanding of "who they are" as a heterogeneous group of social actors.

In the main chapters of the book, thinking through the various methodological challenges of conducting research and further thinking about cultural production and not just cultural representation (Saha 2018), different and diverse understandings emerged about British Asian womanhood. For example, privileging the oral testimonies and memories of older British Asian women, recognizing how knowledge and power can be imbued from one generation to the next by sharing and hearing the stories of first-generation South Asian diasporic migrants, was significant; in and through a focus on the cultural analyses of two films, *Bend It like Beckham* and *Dhan Dhana Dhan Goal*, providing "a view from elsewhere" through a comparative analysis, enabled the vagaries of South Asianness, power, and inequity to become visible; and also, thinking about how younger, second- to third-generation British Asian girls and women, as football players and fans, negotiated their inclusion and exclusion from within the sport vis-à-vis other racial and ethnic groups in postcolonial times exemplified wider debates about the complexities of identity and inequalities. South Asianness cannot be read solely in relation to some intersectional positionings—for example, religion and culture—but demands thinking across other sexual, cultural, geographical, disabled, and queer contexts too. There is so much more to write and understand. This book offers an understanding of South Asian femininity through sport and leisure contexts and addresses a more capacious and intersectional sense of being and becoming that has been relatively absent in the literature so far (Ratna and Samie 2017).

Storying Race, Gender, and the Nation

A deconstruction and reconstruction of the lives and experiences of British Asian women also enabled a rereading of the politics of race, gender, and the nation that retrieved and made visible stories about these women's engagements in walking as a leisure pastime and playing and watching football as a practice of sporting consumption. By focusing on their experiences of sport and leisure, we also see sides to British Asian women that are rarely considered in wider sociological, feminist, and cultural studies literature. Thus, the families and the friends that we make and choose, in and through our sporting and leisure engagements, play a key part in claiming geographical and psychological rights to "our" local spaces of home and belonging (see also Brah 1996). The participants' experiences of sport and leisure culture, therefore, revealed local-global attachments as firmly rooted to England while also seeing them as diasporic actors across time and space. In other words, they walked, kicked, and played in ways that cemented their diasporic orientation to home in the United Kingdom.

The conceptualization of family and friendship is useful to explore further diasporic spaces. It speaks to an enduring sense of who "we" are as a people, as a race, and as a nation across colonial, postcolonial, and imperial histories of divide and rule. This is not to romanticize such friendships or to downplay them as merely insignificant but to recognize that such ties between people can be seen as an important aspect of coming together while, albeit, divided and in tension. For example, this was the case for the British Muslim players at the Women's Islamic Games in Iran in 2001 (see chapter 4), who first felt connected to other Muslim (Afghan) women but later realized they were fractured by wider social forces outside of their control. The hurt being expressed by one of the Afghan players was palpable and could not be easily erased: "Why is your country doing this to us?"

Consider further the imagined "desiness" represented in *Dhan Dhana Dhan Goal* (see chapter 3), uniting an imagined India that is unfractured by deeply rooted historical religious tensions among Hindu, Sikh, and Muslim communities that even during the time of the film's release were experienced as deadly along the Pakistani and Indian border in states such as Gujarat (e.g., the killing of one thousand innocent Muslim civilians in 2002; see Mishra 2012). This team of British Asian men who played for their local football team presented a united and glorified "front," winning "victory" over their local White English opponents and former colonial rulers. Despite differences between the British Asian men in terms of their ethnicity and faith, many of them enjoyed similar leisure pastimes, such as going to the pub and flirting with women, as their "White" competitors did too.

Even in France, for one of the women British Asian players discussed in chapter 4, these lived tensions can manifest through encounters with White English fans, almost instantly leading to jovial celebrations that connect "them" as fans and people. Gender is crucial in this context, enabling a former elite women's football player to pass in a space where the coach of a young British Asian team, despite overt displays of his allegiance (wearing the England shirt), was still seen by other White English fans as an enemy of the nation—that is, a Muslim terrorist. He, therefore, was assumed to be "for" the oppositional Eastern European, Macedonian (White) Muslim opponents of the English men's football squad. The convivial contexts of both sport and leisure settings, as discussed further below, have the potential to bring people together even as they are divided. It is this coming together (in difference) that I consider next.

The Families and Friends We Make and Choose

In this book, I have adopted the concept of family and friends to describe relationships between people and explore the national matrixes of being and belonging. The friends and families we belong to structure our place in the world (across racial "blood" lines and familial and ethnic categorizations) alongside those we play football with, socialize with, go on walks with, and so on across markers of race, ethnicity, gender, sexuality, caste, class, and religion and geographical boundaries of being and belonging. These are the communities we choose and stand together with. This is not to suggest that all friendship or family relationships are positive, as tensions and ambiguities may manifest even among those we see as our political sisters and brethren. However, the act of "communing" together for a particular purpose, with families and friends, can help us survive and move through complex forces of oppression and control.

In chapter 2, for example, the British Asian women enjoy walking together, as it is an extension of their friendship and family connections, having worked together and seen each other's children grow up. The functional nature of their friendships also was crucial to their early experiences of arrival; it provided important connections to help them manage a new life at home with young families as well as to cope with the tough and challenging labor they undertook in the world of work. Over time, while their friendship and family circumstances changed, they spent time together for leisure and pleasure, means through which they continue to see themselves as diasporic citizens at "home" in England and as valued insiders, concomitantly socializing with each other as an expat community in their homes "away from home" in India. Thus, the decisions they make vis-à-vis one another demonstrate the power of communing together to work out their senses of home, belonging, future health, and life aspirations. By focusing on gender in and through this chapter, the voices of women are significant to retrieve not only to contest stereotypical depictions of them as typical older-generation South Asian women but, moreover, to show them as radical "homemakers" actively involved in creating their own senses of home and belonging as long-term settlers, as they walked and literally marked their local spaces of neighborhood and home as "theirs."

In chapter 3, the friendship and family bonds explored in and between the various key characters of *Bend It like Beckham* and *Dhan Dhana Dhan Goal*, respectively, situate the family and local community as important locations for grappling with senses of home and belonging. This is not to say that fictive senses of the "South Asian" community are unimportant, as often, local manifestations of South Asianness speak to such imagined senses of "desiness." For Sunny, a "Hindustani" diasporic sense of being was important to bringing him back—from Western and neoliberal sporting cultures—to his own family and community circles. Conversely, for Jess, her family is viewed as temporarily blocking her from entering a freer sporting world outside the remit of her own South Asian community. Yet both films also show how coming together fosters joy that brings teammates closer irrespective of race, ethnicity, faith, and age. There is hope in both representations: for Jess, reaching her goals of becoming a professional football player and, for Sunny, playing in a successful (predominantly British Asian) team at local levels of the game in England.

In chapter 4, communing together with other football players and fans, on one hand, showed how divides could be superficially transcended—for example, between the Muslim players from

Afghanistan and England and between the British Asian England fan and other White England fans. But, on the other hand, temporary moments of hope, unity, and togetherness did not mean that these divisions were simply overcome. The players at BAFC chose to tackle racism on the field of play and through their rude gal sensibilities, while the British Asian men footballers could not overcome the gendered nature of how they were identified as "Muslim" and other.

A Sporting *and* Academic "Commons"?

Before positing my satirical take on an antiracist "tool kit" (see the epilogue), I want to reflect further on sporting and academic solidarity. Without glossing over the view of friendships and familial bonds as simply enabling, it is worth returning to Lugones's (2003) insights—namely, that sites of "family" and "friendship" (however those relationships are imagined and realized) are also spaces and sites imbued with power, risk, anxiety, tension, and abuse. Thus, I am not suggesting that a sporting or leisure "commons" is essentially a place of choice and liberation. Rather, the communities that place "us" in the world, as friends and family, and the ones we choose to engage with across our lifetimes—sporting, in this case—must always be viewed as complex (Anzaldúa 1987). While tensions are also part of all family and friendship relations (see the preface), I optimistically hold hope for how being and coming together *may* foster loving perceptions, knowing all too well that arrogant perceptions violently divide (see chapter 1). In the different sections of this book, I have spoken to this contradictory context, elucidating inequities, divisions, and discriminations while demonstrating how sport and leisure spaces can be important sites for gaining pleasure and knowledge and creating alliances to carve out new and better futures. It is, arguably, when we struggle to realize "our" utopian futures (see the introduction)—when walking with friends, watching and feeling inspired by films, and enjoying moments of togetherness on and off the football field of play—that hope is generated.

Crossing social divisions as an act of solidarity is increasingly being witnessed in sport—for example, athletes' participation in the Black Lives Matter campaign. From the spectacular to the quotidian, the stories of everyday, local, and somewhat hidden actions of people cannot be underestimated; these stories are powerful and can change lives, raise awareness, and pressure sporting institutions to move beyond tokenistic rhetoric and implement policies to make a "real" change (that is monitored and thus made accountable). I also wish to extend the idea of crossing social identities and geographical spaces to include theoretical crossings to move beyond neoliberal metric cultures embedded in European/Western academic traditions. This culture is damaging: the constant drive to meet ever-increasing targets across several performance indicators that are often conflicting is stretching academics, making collective work tense, and enhancing senses of "publish or peril." I have other kinds of feminist and antiracist dreams, ones that include working with people (however hard that experience can be) across our different roles, positions, disciplinary traditions, and theoretical preferences as an act of solidarity (e.g., see Ratna et al. 2017). It is a personal project I too must work on. Arguably, I believe having difficult dialogues across our social identities, geographic spaces, and academic communities is necessary for creating an "academic commons." These dialogues hold hope that a different future is possible and can be activated in and through our academic activisms.

Conclusion

As this book comes to an end, I want to reiterate that power has contradictory impacts that we feel in our everyday lives and shapes our respective "lots" in life. Writing to these contradictory forces is difficult because, on one hand, I do not want to dismiss pleasure, utopian possibilities, and the power of working with people who are/become allies—who feel kindred to us. But in neoliberal times, and mindful of the devasting impacts of inequality, dehumanization, and discrimination, on the other hand,

I recognize that moments of coming together for the greater good feel remote, and so much more needs to be done in and across our friendship, familial, and academic circles to address social inequities. By telling stories of different British Asian girls and women in and through different sport and leisure contexts, I have provided a rereading of these dynamic forces across the interstices of race, gender, and nation. These stories are important to share. They provide a nuanced, complex, and multifarious re/presentation of British Asianness that at least moves beyond a universalizing single script about "the South Asian woman" (see chapter 1). I hold on to these stories, knowing, as I do, that passing knowledge on from one generation to the next is also an act of solidarity that I share with my children as my parents shared with me.

Epilogue

An Antiracist Feminist Tool Kit

When I began to craft the concluding chapter, I started to see more clearly the relationship among the preface, interludes, and this epilogue: they re/present my erotic—the experiences, thoughts, feelings, and lived insights that say something about my particular place in the world and why I write the way I do and for who. As I could not face writing a preplanned "tool kit" of the "how" and "whys" of my antiracist and feminist approach, which could easily be commodified as an antiracism performative (Ahmed 2006), I wanted to write something in a tongue-in-cheek style—for my own fun and perhaps of the reader too. Moreover, this epilogue (and this book) speaks to a Black, Indigenous, and people of color audience. It is outrightly not made for an oppressive White (feminist) gaze. Through this refusal, I choose to mock instead Whiteness and White professionalism. I no longer choose to deal with White fragility (DiAngelo 2019), knowing also that White, antiracist, and feminist allies may also get that the joke is not funny because it is too "real" to be untrue. Satirically, I have called this piece "Say What?" because I am going to say what also needs to be said as a form of speaking truth to power.

SAY WHAT?

1. Respect your Black, Indigenous, and women of color authors by not eating up their ideas and regurgitating them as your own

original analyses. That means not just citing the work of key Black, Indigenous, and women of color figures (though that is important) but also identifying and acknowledging those writing from these perspectives in the here and now.

2. Don't be lazy. Find those people, cite them, and don't let them be the last to be invited to discussions in areas of their expertise.

3. If a Black, Indigenous, or person of color scholar is talking about Whiteness and you are White, then your life is privileged in a system where you are already the norm. Use your power or go home (and stay in your box). Thank you.

4. If a Black, Indigenous, or person of color tells you that something you did or said was hurtful to them, don't back out of the conversation, suggest that their interpretation is wrong, or listen tokenistically. We see *you*. Respect would follow if the conversation was honest and apologies were given for an offense caused, unintentional or not. Also, slagging us off gets back to us; we see you jokers too.

5. Don't jump on the Black Lives Matter bandwagon—we know you careerists are out there, ready to cash in. Return to number 3: don't sulk, do better.

6. "Check ya self (but don't wreck yourself)"—the one bit of advice I tell others and don't follow myself.

7. Don't write sophisticated critiques about power and social justice and then walk around with your eyes closed to your own complicity and abuse of the system. You should return to number 3.

8. Open your ears and eyes and engage your senses. I am telling you loud and clear. Don't give me crap about "my tone," attitude, or "professionalism." Those terms create a mask to cover social injustice. Just listen and do. Yoda said "Do or do not. There is no try."

9. Please keep your White tears to yourself; I don't want to be burdened with your fragility or guilt. I have so much to do already to challenge the current status quo. Wipe your tears and start the action; I'm too emotionally spent to give you a pat on the back.

10. There are many ways to skin a cat, so the saying goes. My antiracist practice doesn't have to be yours. The antiracist practice must be a pluralized one, but looking out for each other's backs is just how it should be.

Acknowledgments

I began writing the proposal for this book so long ago, it is hard to recall who I spoke to or received advice from at the time. Apologies in advance for missing anyone, but I wanted to extend thanks to certain people whose words of advice have stuck with me. Ben Carrington and Erica Rand were early reviewers of my initial book proposal. Ben made me think about the time it takes to write a book, advice I increasingly learned to accept as time passed by. After all, this book is a personal and not just academic project, so it took time as life happened. Erica, at the time, also made me think about the value of starting the book from where I had ended my initial proposal, thinking further about the politics of family and friendship. From this bit of crucial advice, *A Nation of Family and Friends?* was conceived in its current format.

From these early beginnings, I shelved a drafted manuscript as I took up paid employment in a community rather than academic/ institutional setting. This book would not have seen the light of day if it was not for Jeffrey Montez de Oca, who contacted me in December 2020 to inquire about the progress of the book based on my initial discussions with him from the previous year. Jeffrey, for responding at that moment, for hearing my voice, for giving me early words of support, and for stepping in to help me at a time of need—these are the reasons this book is being published with you and the *Critical Issues in Sport and Society* series at Rutgers University Press. Jeffrey, thank you.

Stanley Thangaraj, dear brother, words cannot express how much I value and cherish you. You remain my first and most engaged reader.

Your comments on earlier drafts were invaluable, giving me the confidence to keep writing. Thanks for getting me and getting the project. I also thank Tricia McGuire-Adams, who also read the entire manuscript and provided feedback on an earlier draft. Moreover, I thank both Stanley and Tricia for their acts of kindness and solidarity.

Others have also been generous with their time, giving me much-needed feedback, courage, and confidence. Kim Toffoletti, I am so grateful to you. Thanks for checking in with me, providing feedback on sections of the book, and generally having my back. Janelle Joseph, having you in my corner gives me great strength. Your critical eye and commentary certainly helped me work through some of the stickier sections of the book. I also thank Kyoung-yim Kim and Katherine Jamieson for your words of encouragement and practice of solidarity. Working with you all and others on different projects at this current moment gives me real joy.

Courtney Szto, thank you for your engagement in my work and for providing critical and thorough feedback. Courtney and the people mentioned above gave me their time, and I am thankful for it.

Thanks also to the team at Rutgers for having faith in the book and to Peter Mickulas and the production team for getting it to the finishing line.

Students also play a key part in my academic imagination, as being able to teach coherently helps me think and write coherently. Critical discussions with doctoral students—in particular, Sukina Khan, Gabby Skeldon, Viji Kuppan, and Chris Webster—all helped me in this respect. I am grateful to have been involved in discussions with these impressive and wonderful individuals.

Families are not always the ones you choose but the ones you make through the good times and bad times. Friends who get me inside and outside of work have given me faith: Bailey Adie, Rachel Ali, Helen Archer, Kelly Bray, and Rhian Jones. I am grateful to you all. Thanks to Shruti and Michael. Finally, to the two people who make everything possible, Ramji and Kesar Ratna, thank you for being unbelievably brilliant parents and for everything you do for Lennie, Saffron, and me.

References

Abdel-Shehid, G., and Kalman-Lamb, N. 2015. "Multiculturalism, Gender and *Bend It like Beckham*." *Social Inclusion* 3 (3): 142–152.

Abraham, M. 2000. *Speaking the Unspeakable: Marital Violence among South Asian Immigrants in the United States*. New Brunswick, N.J.: Rutgers University Press.

Adams, I. 2015. "A Game for Christmas: The Argylls, Saxons, and Football on the Western Front." *International Journal of the History of Sport* 32 (11–12): 1395–1415.

Adjepong, A. 2015. "'We're, like, a Cute Rugby Team': How Whiteness and Heterosexuality Shape Women's Sense of Belonging in Rugby." *International Review for the Sociology of Sport* 52 (2): 209–222.

Ahmad, A. 2011. "British Football: Where Are the British Muslim Female Footballers? Exploring the Connections between Gender, Ethnicity and Islam." *Soccer & Society* 12 (3): 443–456.

Ahmad, W. I. U., and Bradby, H. 2007. "Locating Ethnicity and Health: Exploring Concepts and Contexts." *Sociology of Health and Illness* 29 (9): 795–810.

Ahmed, S. 2006. "The Nonperformativity of Antiracism." *Meridians* 7 (1): 104–126.

———. 2017. *Living a Feminist Life*. Durham, N.C.: Duke University Press.

———. 2021. *Complaint!* Durham, N.C.: Duke University Press.

Albone, T., Martens, L., and Knott, L., dirs. 2010. *Out of the Ashes*. London: Artificial Eye.

Ali, M. 2020. *Decolonising Sociology: A Guide to Theory and Practice*. Cambridge: Polity Press.

Ali, N., Kalra, V. S., and Sayyid, S. 2006. *A Postcolonial People: South Asians in Britain*. London: C. Hurst.

Amin, A. 2002. "Ethnicity and the Multicultural City: Living with Diversity." *Environment and Planning A*, no. 34, 959–980.

———. 2012. *Land of Strangers*. Cambridge: Polity Press.

Amos, V., and Parmar, P. 1984. "Challenging Imperial Feminism." *Feminist Review*, no. 17, 3–19.

Andrews, D. L., and Silk, M. L., eds. 2012. *Sport and Neoliberalism: Politics, Consumption, and Culture*. Philadelphia: Temple University Press.

Anzaldúa, G. 1987. *Borderlands / La Frontera: The New Mestiza*. San Francisco: Aunt Lute Books.

Back, L. 1993. "Race, Identity and Nation within an Adolescent Community in South London." *New Community* 19 (2): 217–233.

———. 1996. *New Ethnicities and Urban Culture: Racisms and Multiculture in Young Lives*. London: UCL Press.

Back, L., Crabbe, T., and Solomos, J. 2001. *The Changing Face of Football: Race, Identity, and Multiculture in the English Game*. Oxford: Berg.

Back, L., Keith, M., Khan, A., Shukra, K., and Solomos, J. 2002. "New Labour's White Heart: Politics, Multiculturalism and the Return of Assimilation." *Political Quarterly* 73 (4): 445–454.

Banerjea, N., Dasgupta, D., Dasgupta, R. K., and Grant, J. M. 2018. *Friendship as Social Justice Activism: Critical Solidarities in a Global Perspective*. Calcutta: Seagull Books.

Barker-Ruchti, N., Barker, D., Sattler, S., Gerber, M., and Uwe, P. 2013. "Sport—'It's Just Healthy': Locating Healthism within Discourses of Social Integration." *Journal of Ethnic and Migration Studies* 39 (5): 759–772.

Bey, M. 2019. *Them Goon Rules: Fugitive Essays on Radical Black Feminism*. Tucson: University of Arizona Press.

Bhambra, G. K. 2007. *Rethinking Modernity: Postcolonialism and the Sociological Imagination*. Basingstoke, U.K.: Palgrave.

———. 2014. *Connected Sociologies*. London: Bloomsbury.

Bhambra, G. K., Gebrial, D., and Nişancıoğlu, K., eds. 2018. *Decolonising the University*. London: Pluto Press.

Bhattacharya, G. 2018. *Re-thinking Racial Capitalism: Questions of Reproduction and Survival*. Boulder, Colo.: Rowman & Littlefield.

Bhattacharya, G., Elliot-Cooper, A., Balani, S., Nişancıoğlu, K., Koram, K., Gebrial, D., El-Enany, N., and de Noronha, L. 2021. *Empire's End Game: Racism and the British State*. London: Pluto Press.

Bowes, A. M., and Domokos, T. M. 1993. "South Asian Women and Health Services: A Study in Glasgow." *New Community* 19 (4): 611–626.

Boykoff, J., and Carrington, B. 2019. "Sporting Dissent: Colin Kaepernick, NFL Activism, and Media Framing Contexts." *International Review for the Sociology of Sport* 55 (7): 829–849.

Brackenridge, C. 2001. *Spoilsport: Understanding and Preventing Sexual Exploitation in Sport.* London: Routledge.

Brah, A. 1983. "'Race' and 'Culture' in the Gendering of Labour Markets: South Asian Young Muslim Women and the Labour Market." *New Community* 19 (3): 441–458.

———. 1996. *Cartographies of Diaspora: Contesting Identities.* London: Routledge.

———. 1999. "The Scent of Memory: Strangers, Our Own, and Others." *Feminist Review* 61 (1): 4–26.

Brown, L. E. C. 2017. "Post-colonial Feminism, Black Feminism and Sport." In *The Palgrave Handbook of Feminism and Sport, Leisure and Physical Education*, edited by L. Mansfield, J. Caudwell, B. Wheaton, and B. Watson, 479–495. London: Palgrave Macmillan.

———. 2022. "NASSS Public Statement on Taking Athletes as Political Prisoners." NASSS. Accessed January 3, 2023. https://nasss.org/wp-content/uploads/2022/12/NASSS-Condems-Athletes-Political-Prisoners.pdf.

———. Forthcoming. *Say Her Name.* New Brunswick, N.J.: Rutgers University Press.

Burdsey, D. 2004. "Obstacle Race? 'Race,' Racism, and the Recruitment of British Asian Professional Footballers." *Patterns of Prejudice* 38 (3): 279–299.

———. 2006. "'If I Ever Play Football, Dad, Can I Play for England or India?' British Asians, Sport, and Diasporic National Identities." *Sociology* 40 (1): 11–28.

———, ed. 2011. *Race, Ethnicity, and Football: Persisting Debates and Emergent Issues.* London: Routledge.

———. 2021. *Racism and English Football: For Club and Country.* London: Routledge.

Burdsey, D., and Randhawa, K. 2012. "How Can Professional Football Clubs Be Welcoming and Inclusive Spaces for British Asian Fans?" *Journal of Policy Research in Tourism, Leisure and Events* 4 (1): 105–111.

Burdsey, D., Thangaraj, S., and Dudrah, R. 2013. "Playing through Time and Space: Sport and South Asian Diasporas." Special issue, *South Asian Popular Culture* 11 (3).

Butler, J. 1990. *Gender Trouble: Feminism and the Subversion of Identity*. New York: Routledge.

Cahn, S. K. 1994. *Coming on Strong: Gender and Sexuality in Twentieth Century Women's Sport*. Cambridge, Mass.: Harvard University Press.

Campbell, P. 2020. *Football, Retirement and Career Transitions for Black Ex-Professional Footballers: From Being Idolised to Stacking Shelves*. Bingley, U.K.: Emerald.

Carrington, B. 1998. "Sport, Masculinity, and Black Cultural Resistance." *Journal of Sport and Social Issues* 22 (3): 275–298.

———. 2010. *Race, Sport and Politics: The Sporting Black Diaspora*. Los Angeles: Sage.

———. 2012. "Introduction: Sport Matters." *Ethnic and Racial Studies* 35 (6): 961–970.

Carter, T. 2007. "Family Networks, State Interventions and the Experience of Transnational Cuban Sports Migration." *International Review for the Sociology of Sport* 42 (4): 371–389.

Carter-Francique, A., and Olushola, J. 2016. "Women Coaches of Color: Examining the Effects of Intersectionality." In *Women in Sports Coaching*, edited by N. Le Voi, 81–94. London: Routledge.

Carter-Francique, A., and Richardson, M. F. 2016. "Controlling Media, Controlling Access." *Race, Gender and Class* 23 (1–2): 7–33.

Caudwell, J. 1999. "Women's Football in the United Kingdom: Theorizing Gender and Unpacking the Butch Lesbian." *Journal of Sport and Social Issues* 23 (4): 390–402.

———. 2009. "*Girlfight* and *Bend It like Beckham*: Screening Women, Sport and Sexuality." *Journal of Lesbian Studies* 13 (3): 255–271.

Caudwell, J., Healy, J., and Ratna, A. 2023. "Women Footballers in the United Kingdom: Feminism, Misogynoir, and Hate Crime." In *Racism and Hate Crime in Football*, edited by I. Zempi and I. Awan, 134–152. Cambridge: Polity Press.

Chandra, S. 2020. "Decolonizing the Orgasm: Caste, Whiteness and Knowledge Production at the 'End of Empire.'" *South Asia: Journal of South Asian Studies* 43 (6): 1179–1195.

Chatterjee, S. 2021. "The 'Good Indian Queer Woman' and the Family: Politics of Normativity and Travails of (Queer) Representation." *South Asian Popular Culture* 19 (2): 177–192.

Chawansky, M., and Mitra, P. 2015. "Family Matters: Studying the Role of the Family through the Eyes of Girls in a SfD Programme in India." *Sport in Society* 18 (8): 983–984.

Chowdhury, E., and Phillipose, L. 2016. *Dissident Friendships: Feminism, Imperialism, and Transnational Solidarity*. Champaign: Illinois University Press.

Çidam, C. 2017. "Unruly Practices: Gezi Protest and the Politics of Friendship." *New Political Science* 39 (3): 369–392.

Coalter, F. 2013. *Sport for Development: What Game Are We Playing?* London: Routledge.

Coakley, J. 2011. "Youth Sports: What Counts as 'Positive Development?'" *Journal of Sport and Social Issues* 35 (3): 306–324.

Cole, C. L., and Hribar, A. 1995. "Celebrity Feminism: Nike Style Post-Fordism, Transcendence, and Consumer Power." *Sociology of Sport Journal* 12 (4): 347–369.

Collins, M. 2012. "Rabindranath Tagore and the Politics of Friendship." *South Asia: Journal of South Asian Studies* 35 (1): 118–142.

Collins, P. H. 2000. *Black Feminist Thought: Knowledge, Consciousness, and the Politics of Empowerment*. 2nd ed. New York: Routledge.

Connell, R. 2013. "Using Southern Theory: Decolonising Social Thought in Theory, Research, and Application." *Planning Theory* 13 (2): 210–233.

Conrad, J. 1899. *Heart of Darkness*. Claremont, Calif.: Cayote Canyon Press.

Crenshaw, K. 1989. "Demarginalizing the Intersections of Race and Sex: A Black Feminist Critique of Antidiscrimination Doctrine, Feminist Theory and Antiracist Politics." *University of Chicago Legal Forum* 1 (8): 139–167.

Crenshaw, K. W., Ritchie, A. J., Anspach, R., Gilmer, R., and Harris, L. 2015. "Say Her Name: Resisting Police Brutality Against Women." Centre for Intersectionality and Social Policy Studies. https://scholarship.law.columbia.edu/faculty_scholarship/3226.

Datta, S. 2000. "Globalisation and Representations of Women in Indian Cinema." *Social Scientist* 28 (3–4): 71–82.

Dave, N. 2012. *Queer Activism in India: A Story in the Anthropology of Ethics*. Durham, N.C.: Duke University Press.

Davies, A. 2017. "Exile in the Homeland? Anti-colonialism, Subaltern Geographies and the Politics of Friendship in Early Twentieth Century Pondicherry, India." *Environment and Planning D: Society and Space* 35 (3): 457–474.

de Jong, S., Icaza, R., and Rutazibwa, O. 2018. *Decolonization and Feminisms in Global Teaching and Learning.* London: Routledge.

Desai, J. 2004. *Beyond Bollywood: The Cultural Politics of the South Asian Diaspora.* New York: Routledge.

Desai, P., and Sekhon, P. 2003. *Red Threads: The South Asian Queer Connection in Photographs.* London: Millivrés Prowler Group.

Devika, J., and Thampi, B. V. 2011. "Mobility towards Work and Politics for Women in Kerala State, Kerala: A View from the Histories of Gender and Space." *Modern Asian Studies* 45 (5): 1147–1175.

DiAngelo, R. J. 2019. *White Fragility: Why It's So Hard for White People to Talk about Racism.* Boston: Beacon Press.

Dudrah, R. K. 2006. *Sociology Goes to the Movies.* London: SAGE.

Emejulu, A. 2022. *Fugitive Feminism.* London: Silver Press.

Entine, J. 2000. *Taboo: Why Black Athletes Dominate Sports and Why We're Afraid to Talk about It.* New York: PublicAffairs.

Farooq, S. 2011. "'Tough Talk,' Muscular Islam and Football: Young British Pakistani Muslim Masculinities." In *Race, Ethnicity, and Football: Persisting Debates and Emergent Issues*, edited by D. Burdsey, 145–162. London: Routledge.

Ferguson, R. A. 2003. *Aberrations in Black: Toward a Queer of Color Critique.* Minneapolis: University of Minnesota Press.

Finney, C., and Mapp, R. 2014. "The *Boom* Interview: Outdoor Afro." *Journal of California* 4 (3): 76–85.

Fletcher, T. 2011. "The Making of English Cricket Cultures: Empire, Globalisation and (Post) Colonialism." *Sport in Society* 14 (1): 17–36.

Frankenberg, R. 1993. *White Women, Race Matters: The Social Construction of Whiteness.* Minneapolis: University of Minnesota Press.

Fukuyama, F. 1992. *The End of History and the Last Man.* New York: Penguin Random House.

Fullagar, S., and O'Brien, W. 2014. "Social Recovery and the Move beyond Deficit Models of Depression: A Feminist Analysis of Mid-life Women's Self-Care Practices." *Social Science & Medicine* 117 (C): 116–124.

Fullagar, S., O'Brien, W., and Pavlidis, A. 2019. *Feminism and a Vital Politics of Depression and Recovery*. Cham, Switzerland: Palgrave Macmillan.

Gilroy, P. 2004. *After Empire: Melancholia or Convivial Culture?* Abingdon, U.K.: Routledge.

Giroux, H. 2000. "Public Pedagogy as Cultural Politics: Stuart Hall and the Crisis of Culture." *Cultural Studies* 14 (2): 341–360.

———. 2003. "Spectacles of Race and Pedagogies of Denial: Anti-Black Racist Pedagogy under the Reign of Neoliberalism." *Communication Education* 52 (3–4): 191–211.

Giulianotti, R., and Robertson, R. 2009. *Globalization and Football*. London: SAGE.

Gopinath, G. 2005. *Impossible Desires: Queer Diasporas and South Asian Public Cultures*. Durham, N.C.: Duke University Press.

———. 2018. *Unruly Visions: The Aesthetic Practices of Queer Diaspora*. Durham, N.C.: Duke University Press.

Gozdecka, D. A., Ercan, S. A., and Kmak, M. 2014. "From Multiculturalism to Postmulticulturalism: Trends and Paradoxes." *Journal of Sociology* 50 (1): 51–64.

Grewal, I. 1996. *Home and Harem: Nation, Gender, Empire, and the Cultures of Travel*. London: Leicester University Press.

Grosz, E. 1994. *Volatile Bodies: Towards a Corporeal Feminism*. Bloomington: Indiana University Press.

Gupta, A., and Ferguson, J. 1992. "Beyond 'Culture': Space, Identity, and the Politics of Difference." *Cultural Anthropology* 7 (1): 6–23.

Hall, S. 1996. "New Ethnicities." In *Critical Dialogues in Cultural Studies*, edited by K.-H. Chen and D. Morley, 452–467. London: Routledge.

Hall, S., Massey, D., and Rustin, M., eds. 2015. *After Neoliberalism: The Kilburn Manifesto*. London: Lawrence & Wishart.

Harney, S., and Moten, F. 2013. *The Undercommons: Fugitive Planning and Black Study*. Wivenhoe, U.K.: Minor Compositions.

Harris, J. 2005. "The Image Problem in Women's Football." *Journal of Sport and Social Issues* 29 (2): 184–197.

Hartill, M. 2009. "The Sexual Abuse of Boys in Male Organised Sports." *Men and Masculinities* 12 (2): 225–249.

Hartmann, D. 2003. "What Can We Learn from Sport If We Take Sport Seriously as a Racial Force? Lessons from C.L.R. James's *Beyond a Boundary*." *Ethnic and Racial Studies* 26 (3): 451–483.

Hoare, N. 2018. "Anticolonialism and the Politics of Friendship in New Zealand's Pacific." *History Australia* 15 (3): 540–558.

hooks, b. 1992. "Eating the Other: Desire and Resistance." In *Black Looks: Race and Representation*, 21–39. Boston: South End Press.

Huntingdon, S. P. 1996. *The Clash of Civilizations and the Remaking of World Order*. London: Simon & Schuster.

Iimonen, K. 2019. "Identity Politics Revisited: On Audre Lorde, Intersectionality, and Mobilizing Writing Styles." *European Journal of Women's Studies* 26 (1): 7–22.

Jackson, E. 2020. "Bowling Together? Practices of Belonging and Becoming in a London Tenpin Bowling League." *Sociology* 54 (3): 518–533.

James, C. L. R. 2013. *Beyond a Boundary*. 50th Anniversary ed. Durham, N.C.: Duke University Press.

Jamieson, K. 1998. "Reading Nancy Lopez: Decoding Representations of Race, Class and Sexuality." *Sociology of Sport Journal*, no. 15, 343–358.

———. 2003. "Occupying a Middle Space: Toward a Mestiza Sport Studies." *Sociology of Sport Journal*, no. 20, 1–16.

Jamieson, K., and Choi, Y. 2017. "Lorena 'La Reina' Ochoa: Disidentifying towards a Brown Commons." In Ratna and Samie, *Race, Gender and Sport*, 171–188.

Jha, S., and Kurian, A. 2018. *New Feminisms in South Asia: Disrupting the Discourse through Social Media, Film and Literature*. New York: Routledge.

Jones, H., Gunaratnam, Y., Jackson, E., Davis, W., Dhaliwal, S., Forkert, K. Bhattacharya, G., and Saltus, R. 2017. *Go Home? The Politics of Immigration Controversies*. Manchester: Manchester University Press.

Joseph, J. 2017. *Sport in the Black Atlantic: Cricket, Canada and the Caribbean Diaspora*. Manchester: Manchester University Press.

Karkazis, K., and Jordan-Young, R. M. 2018a. "The Powers of Testosterone: Obscuring Race and Regional Bias in the Regulation of Women Athletes." *Feminist Formations* 30 (2): 1–39.

———. 2018b. "The Treatment of Caster Semenya Shows Athletes' Bias against Women of Colour." *Guardian*, April 26, 2018. https://www

.theguardian.com/commentisfree/2018/apr/26/testosterone-ruling -women-athletes-caster-semanya-global-south.

Kawale, R. 2003. "A Kiss Is Just a Kiss . . . or Is It? South Asian Lesbian and Bisexual Women and the Construction of Space." In *South Asian Women in the Diaspora*, edited by N. Puwar and P. Raghuram, 181–200. London: Routledge.

Kennedy, H. 2019. *Misjustice: How British Law Is Failing Women*. London: Penguin Random House.

Khubchandani, K. 2020. *Ishtyle: Accenting Gay Indian Nightlife*. Ann Arbor: University of Michigan Press.

Kilvington, D. 2013. "British Asians, Covert Racism and Exclusion in English Professional Football." *Culture Unbound: Journal of Current Cultural Research* 5 (4): 587–606.

Kim, K.-Y. 2013. "Translation with Abusive Fidelity: Methodological Issues in Translating Media Texts about Korean LPGA Players." *Sociology of Sport Journal* 30 (3): 340–358.

King, R., ed. 2014. *Asian American Athletes in Sport and Society*. New York: Routledge.

King, S. 2008. "What's Queer about (Queer) Sport Sociology Now? A Review Essay." *Sociology of Sport Journal* 25 (4): 419–442.

———. 2009. "Homonormativity and Politics of Race: Reading Sheryl Swoopes." *Journal of Lesbian Studies* 13 (3): 272–290.

Krane, V. 1996. "Lesbians in Sport: Towards Acknowledgement and Understanding and Theory." *Journal of Sport and Exercise Psychology* 18 (3): 237–246.

Kumm, B. E., and Johnson, C. W. 2018. "In the Garden of Domestic Dystopia: Racial Delirium and Playful Interference." *Leisure Studies* 37 (6): 692–705.

Kuppan, V. 2018. "Crippin' Blackness: Narratives of Disabled People of Colour from Slavery to Trump." In *The Fire Now: Anti-racism in Times of Explicit Racism*, edited by A. Johnson, R. Joseph-Salisbury, and B. Kumunge, 60–73. London: Zed.

———. 2022. "'But We All Wear the Same Shirt, Don't We?' Football Fan Culture and the Intersections of 'Race,' Disability and Gender." Unpublished PhD thesis, Leeds Beckett University.

Kyeremeh, S. 2019. "Whitening Italian Sport: The Construction of 'Italianness' in National Sporting Fields." *International Review for the Sociology of Sport* 55 (8): 1136–1151.

Laker, A., ed. 2012. *The Sociology of Sport and Physical Education: An Introductory Reader*. London: Routledge.

Laursen, O. B. 2019. "Anti-colonialism, Terrorism and 'the Politics of Friendship': Virendrathnath Chattopahhyaya and the European Anarchist Movement, 1910–1927." *Anarchist Studies* 27 (1): 47–62.

Lenneis, V., and Agergaard, S. 2018. "Enacting and Resisting the Politics of Belonging through Leisure: The Debate about Gender-Segregated Swimming Sessions Targeting Muslim Women in Denmark." *Leisure Studies* 37 (6): 706–720.

Lentin, A., and Titley, G. 2011. *The Crisis in Multiculturalism: Racism in a Neoliberal Age*. London: Zed Books.

Leseth, A. B. 2014. "Experiences of Moving: A History of Women and Sport in Tanzania." *Sport in Society* 17 (3): 479–491.

Littler, J., and Emejulu, A. 2019. "We Do Not Have to Be Vicious, Competitive, or Managerial." *Soundings*, no. 73, 73–86.

Lorde, A. (1984) 2007. *Sister Outsider: Essays and Speeches*. Berkeley, Calif.: Ten Speed Press.

Lowe, L. 2015. *The Intimacies of Four Continents*. Durham, N.C.: Duke University Press.

Lugones, M. A. 2003. *Pilgrimages/Peregrinajes: Theorizing Coalition against Multiple Oppressions*. Lanham, Md.: Rowman & Littlefield.

Lusted, J. 2009. "Playing Games with 'Race': Understanding Resistance to 'Race' Equality Initiatives in English Local Football Governance." *Soccer & Society* 10 (6): 722–739.

Mujumdar, D. C. 1950. "The Encyclopedia of Indian Physical Culture." Physical Culture Study. Accessed August 13, 2022. https://physicalculturestudy.com/2014/12/22/the-encyclopedia-of-indian-physical-culture/.

Manalansan, M. 2003. *Global Divas: Filipino Gay Men in the Diaspora*. Durham, N.C.: Duke University Press.

Mani, V., and Krishnamurthy, M. 2016. "Sociology of Sport: India." In *Sociology of Sport: A Global Subdiscipline in Review*, vol. 9, edited by K. Young, 37–57. Bingley, U.K.: Emerald Group.

———. 2018. "Making a Locality: The Politics of Land and Football in North Kerala." *Leisure Studies* 37 (6): 721–734.

Mankekar, P. 1999. *Screening Culture, Viewing Politics: An Ethnography of Television, Womanhood and Nation in Postcolonial India.* Durham, N.C.: Duke University Press.

Mansfield, L., and Rich, E. 2013. "Public Health Pedagogy, Border Crossings, and Health at Every Size." *Critical Public Health* 23 (3): 356–370.

Mashereghi, S. 2021. "Decolonial Re-existence and Sports: Stories of Afghan Youth in Sweden." Unpublished PhD diss., Malmö University. https://mau.diva-portal.org/smash/record.jsf?pid=diva2%3A1596567&dswid=4705.

McDonald, M. 2009. "Dialogues on Whiteness, Leisure and (Anti)Racism." *Journal of Leisure Research* 41 (1): 5–21.

McGuire-Adams, T. D. 2019. "Decolonizing Sport Sociology Is Not a 'Metaphor': Decentering Colonialism, Unsettling Whiteness, and Indigenizing Sport Sociology." Plenary Session at the North American Sociology of Sport Association's annual conference, Sport Sociology and the Responsibility of Decolonial Praxis: Decolonizing Minds, Indigenizing Hearts, Virginia Beach, Va., November 2019.

———. 2020a. *Indigenous Feminist Gikendaasowin (Knowledge): Decolonization through Physical Activity.* Cham, Switzerland: Palgrave Macmillan.

———. 2020b. "Paradigm Shifting: Centering Indigenous Research Methodologies, an Anishinaabe Perspective." *Qualitative Research in Sport, Exercise and Health* 12 (1): 34–47.

———. 2021. "Settler Allies Are Made, Not Self-Proclaimed: Unsettling Conversations for Non-Indigenous Researchers and Educators Involved in Indigenous Health." *Health Education Journal* 80 (7): 761–772.

McGuire-Adams, T., Joseph, J., Peers, D., Eales, L., Bridel, W., Chen., C., Hamdon, E., and Kingsley, B. 2022. "Awakening to Elsewhere: Collectively Restoring Embodied Experiences of (Be)Longing." *Sociology of Sport Journal* 39 (4): 313–322.

McKittrick, K. 2015. *Slyvia Wynter: On Being Human as Praxis.* Durham, N.C.: Duke University Press.

McRobbie, A. 1991. *Feminism and Youth Culture: From Jackie to Just Seventeen.* Basingstoke, U.K.: Palgrave Macmillan.

Menon, N. 2009. "Sexuality, Caste, Governmentality: Contests over 'Gender' in India." *Feminist Review* 91:94–112.

Mignolo, W. 2000. *Local Histories / Global Designs: Coloniality, Subaltern Knowledges, and Border Thinking.* Princeton, N.J.: Princeton University Press.

Mirza, H. S. 2008. *Race, Gender, and Educational Desire: Why Black Women Succeed and Fail.* London: Routledge.

Mishra, P. 2012. "The Gujarat Massacre: New India's Blood Rite." *Guardian,* March 14, 2012. https://www.theguardian.com/commentisfree/2012/mar/14/new-india-gujarat-massacre.

Mitra, P. 2009. "Challenging Stereotypes: The Case of Muslim Female Boxers in Bengal." *International Journal of the History of Sport* 26 (12): 1840–1851.

———. 2018. "Dutee Chand: It Was Her Grit That Kept Dutee Going." *Times of India,* August 30, 2018. https://timesofindia.indiatimes.com/sports/asian-games/it-was-her-grit-that-kept-dutee-going/articleshow/65606341.cms.

Mohanty, C. T. 1984. "Under Western Eyes: Feminist Scholarship and Colonial Discourses." *boundary 2* 12 (3): 333–358.

———. 2003. *Feminism without Borders: Decolonizing Theory, Practicing Solidarity.* Durham, N.C.: Duke University Press.

Montegary, L. 2018. *Familiar Perversions: The Racial, Sexual, and Economic Politics of LGBT Families.* New Brunswick, N.J.: Rutgers University Press.

Mowatt, R., French, B. H., and Malebranche, D. A. 2013. "Black/Female/Body: *Hypervisibility* and *Invisibility.*" *Journal of Leisure Research* 45 (5): 644–660.

Munford, R., and Waters, R. 2014. *Feminism and Popular Culture: Investigating the Postfeminism Mystique.* London: IB Taurus.

Muñoz, J. E. 2009. *Cruising Utopia: The Then and There of Queer Futurity.* New York: New York University Press.

Naganathan, R., Gupta, D., and Prasad, R. 2021. "Connotation of Leisure and Leisure Activities among Urban Middle-Class Working Women." *Leisure Studies* 40 (6): 837–853.

Nanayakkara, S. 2012. "Crossing Boundaries and Changing Identities: Empowering South Asian Women through Sport and Physical Activity." *International Journal of the History of Sport* 29 (13): 1885–1906.

Nayak, A. 2018. "Purging the Nation: Race, Conviviality, and Embodied Encounters in the Lives of Bangladeshi Muslim Young Women." *Transactions of the British Institute of British Geographers* 42 (2): 289–302.

Nazroo, J. 1997. *The Health of Britain's Ethnic Minorities*. London: Policy Studies Institute.

Nazroo, J., and Bécares, L. 2021. *Ethnic Inequalities in Covid-19 Mortality: A Consequence of Persistent Racism*. London: Runnymeade Trust (Runnymeade / CoDE Briefings).

Neal, S., Bennett, K., Cochrane, A., and Mohan, G. 2019. "Community *and* Conviviality: Informal Social Life in Multicultural Places." *Sociology* 53 (1): 69–86.

Ong, A. 1999. *Flexible Citizenship: The Cultural Logic of Transnationality*. Durham, N.C.: Duke University Press.

Orwell, G. 1945. "The Sporting Spirit." Orwell.ru. Accessed July 4, 2022. http://www.orwell.ru/library/articles/spirit/english/e_spirit.

Owton, H. 2016. *Sexual Abuse in Sport: A Qualitative Case-Study*. London: Springer International.

Paik, S. 2019. "Dalit Women's Agency and Phule-Ambedkarite Feminism." In *Dalit Feminist Theory: A Reader*, edited by S. Arya and A. S. Rathore, 65–87. London: Routledge.

Patel, P. 1997. "Third Wave Feminism and Black Women's Activism." In *Black British Feminism: A Reader*, edited by H. S. Mirza, 255–268. London: Routledge.

Phillips, D. 2006. "Parallel Lives? Challenging Discourses of British Muslim Self-Segregation." *Environment and Planning D: Society and Space* 24 (1): 25–40.

———. 2010. "Minority Ethnic Segregation, Integration and Citizenship: A European Perspective." *Journal of Ethnic and Migration Studies* 36 (2): 209–225.

Phillips, R., Chambers, C., Ali, N., Diprose, K., and Karmakar, I. 2021. *Storying Relationships: Young British Muslims Speak and Write about Sex and Love*. London: Bloomsbury.

Puar, J. 2007. *Terrorist Assemblages: Homonationalism in Queer Times*. Durham, N.C.: Duke University Press.

Puwar, N. 2004. *Space Invaders: Race, Gender and Bodies Out of Place*. Oxford: Berg.

————. 2012. "Mediations on Making *Aaj Kaal.*" *Feminist Review* 100 (1): 124–141.

Puwar, N., and Raghuram, P., eds. 2003. *South Asian Women in the Diaspora.* Oxford: Berg.

Qureshi, K. 2016. "Shehri (City) Brides between Indian Punjab and the UK: Transnational Hypergamy, Sikh's Women's Agency and Gendered Geographies of Power." *Journal of Ethnic and Migration Studies* 47 (7): 1216–1228.

Radice, M. 2016. "Unpacking Intercultural Conviviality in Multiethnic Commercial Streets." *Journal of Intercultural Studies* 37 (5): 432–448.

Rallins, K. N. 2022. "Self-Representation of Black Queer Athletes in the WNBA: Resistance to Misogynoir and Heteronormativity in Women's Basketball." Unpublished PhD thesis, DePaul University. https://via .library.depaul.edu/etd/323.

Ramji, H. 2006. "'Journeys of Difference': The Use of Migratory Narratives among British Hindu Gujaratis." *Ethnic and Racial Studies* 29 (4): 702–724.

Rana, J. 2017. "Ladies-Only! Empowerment and Comfort in Gender-Segregated Kickboxing in the Netherlands." In Ratna and Samie, *Race, Gender and Sport*, 148–168.

Ransom, A. J. 2014. "Bollywood Goes to the Stadium: Gender, National Identity, and Sport Film in Hindi." *Journal of Film and Video* 66 (4): 34–59.

Ratna, A. 2007. "A Fair Game: British-Asian Female's Experiences of Racism in Women's Football." In *Women, Football and Europe: Histories, Equity and Experience*, edited by J. Magee, J. Caudwell, K. Liston, and S. Scraton, 77–96. Eastbourne, U.K.: Meyer and Meyer.

————. 2008. "British Asian Females' Racialised and Gendered Experiences of Identity and Women's Football." Unpublished thesis, University of Brighton.

————. 2010. "'Taking the Power Back!' the Politics of British-Asian Female Football Players." *Young* 18 (2): 117–132.

————. 2011. "'Who Wants to Make Aloo Gobi When You Can Bend It like Beckham?' British Asian Females and Their Racialised Experiences of Gender and Identity in Women's Football." *Soccer & Society* 12 (3): 382–401.

———. 2013. "Intersectional Plays of Identity: The Experiences of British Asian Female Footballers." *Sociological Research Online* 18 (1): 108–117.

———. 2014. "'Who Are Ya?' The National Identities and Belongings of British Asian Football Fans." *Patterns of Prejudice* 48 (3): 286–308.

———. 2017a. "Black Women, Black Voices: The Contribution of a Spivakian and Black Feminist Analysis to Studies of Sport and Leisure." In *Sport, Leisure and Social Justice*, edited by J. Long, T. Fletcher, and B. Watson, 153–167. London: Routledge.

———. 2017b. "No Racism Here Then? Wo/men's Football in the UK and the Case of Eniola Aluko." Media Diversified, October 26, 2017. https://mediadiversified.org/2017/10/26/no-racism-here-then-womens-football-in-the-uk-and-the-case-of-aniola-aluko/.

———. 2017c. "'Using the Pen as a Weapon': The Resistance of an Outsider Within." In Ratna and Samie, *Race, Gender and Sport*, 109–125.

———. 2017d. "Walking for Leisure: The Translocal Lives of First-Generation Gujarati Indian Men and Women." *Leisure Studies* 36 (5): 618–632.

———. 2018. "Not Just Merely Different: Travelling Theories, Postfeminism, and the Racialized Politics of Women of Color." *Sociology of Sport Journal* 35 (30): 197–206.

———. 2019. "Hierarchical Assemblages of Citizenship and Belonging: The Pedestrian Speech Acts of British Gujarati Indian Walkers." *Sociology* 54 (1): 159–180.

Ratna, A., Lawrence, S., and Partington, J. 2015. "'Getting Inside the Wicket': Strategies for the Social Inclusion of British Pakistani Muslim Cricketers." *Journal of Policy Research in Tourism, Leisure and Events* 8 (1): 1–15.

Ratna, A., and Samie, S. F., eds. 2017. *Race, Gender and Sport: The Politics of Ethnic "Other" Girls and Women*. London: Routledge.

Ratna, A., Samie, S. F., Jamieson, K., and Thangaraj, S. 2017. "Learning Lessons from the Politics of Ethnic 'Others.'" In *The Palgrave Handbook of Feminism and Sport, Leisure and Physical Education*, edited by L. Mansfield, J. Caudwell, B. Wheaton, and B. Watson, 627–648. London: Palgrave Macmillan.

Razack, S. 2022. "Joy as a Mode of Resistance: An Examination of Black Girl Hockey Club's Ongoing Quest for Racial Justice." Unpublished PhD thesis, University of Toronto.

Razack, S., and Joseph, J. 2020. "Misogynoir in Women's Sports Media: Race, Nation and Diaspora in the Representation of Naomi Osaka." *Media, Culture and Society* 43 (2): 291–308.

Redhead, S. 1997. *Subcultures to Clubcultures: An Introduction to Popular Cultural Studies.* Oxford: Blackwell.

Richards, R. 2017. "'What's Your Name, Where Are You From, and What Have You Had?' Utopian Memories of Leeds Acid House Culture in Two Acts." In *The Oxford Handbook of Music-Making and Leisure*, edited by R. Mantie and D. Smith, 385–404. New York: Oxford University Press.

Rings, G. 2011. "Questions of Identity: Cultural Encounters in Gurinder Chadha's *Bend It like Beckham.*" *Journal of Film and Television* 39 (3): 114–123.

Rose, G. 1993. *Feminism & Geography: The Limits of Geographical Knowledge.* Minneapolis: University of Minnesota Press.

Roy, A. 1997. *The God of Small Things.* New Delhi: IndiaInk.

———. 2017. *The Ministry of Utmost Happiness.* London: Hamish Hamilton.

Saad, L. 2020. *Me and White Supremacy: How to Recognise Your Privilege, Combat Racism and Change the World.* London: Quercus.

Saeed, A., and Kilvington, D. 2011. "British-Asians and Racism within Contemporary English Football." *Soccer & Society* 12 (5): 602–612.

Saha, A. 2018. *Race and the Cultural Industries.* Cambridge: Polity Press.

Samie, S. F. 2013. "Hetero-sexy Self/Body Work and Basketball: Invisible Sporting Women of Pakistani Muslim Heritage." *Journal of South Asian Popular Culture* 11 (3): 257–270.

———. 2017. "De/Colonising 'Sporting Muslim Women': Postcolonial Feminist Reflections on the Dominant Portrayal of Sporting Muslim Women in Academic Research, Public Forums and Mediated Representations." In Ratna and Samie, *Race, Gender and Sport*, 35–62.

Samie, S. F., Johnson, A. J., Huffman, A. M., and Hillyer, S. J. 2015. "Voices of/on Empowerment: Women from the Global South Re/Negotiating Empowerment and the Global Sports Mentoring Programme." *Sport in Society* 18 (8): 923–937.

Samie, S. F., and Sehlikoglu, S. 2015. "Strange, Incompetent and Out-of-Place: Media, Muslim Women and the London 2012 Olympics." *Feminist Media Studies* 15 (3): 363–381.

Santa Cruz Feminist of Color Collective. 2014. "Building on 'the Edge of Each Other's Battles': A Feminist of Color Multidimensional Lens." *Hypatia* 29 (1): 23–40.

Schneider, A.-K. 2019. "The Politics of Friendship and the Gendering of Discourse in Anne Enright's *The Gathering*." *College Literature: A Journal of Critical Literary Studies* 46 (3): 659–683.

Scraton, S., and Watson, B. 1998. "Gendered Cities: Women and Public Leisure Spaces in the 'Postmodern City.'" *Leisure Studies* 17 (2): 123–137.

Shahzadi, U. 2018. "The Body Triad, Whiteness and Agency: The Not-So-Sporty Experiences of Punjabi-Canadian Women." Master's dissertation, University of Toronto.

Sharma, S., Hutnyk, J., and Sharma, A. 1996. *Dis-orienting Rhythms: The Politics of the New Asian Dance Music.* London: Zed Books.

Sharpe, C. 2016. *In the Wake: On Blackness and Being.* Durham, N.C.: Duke University Press.

Sharpe, J. 2005. "Gender, Nation, and Globalisation in Monsoon Wedding and Dilwale Dulhania Le Jayenge." *Meridians: Feminism, Race, Transnationalism* 6 (1): 58–81.

Simpson, L. B. 2016. "Indigenous Resurgence and Co-resistance." *Critical Ethnic Studies* 2 (2): 19–34.

Sivanandan, A. 2008. *Catching History on the Wing: Race, Culture and Globalisation.* London: Pluto Press.

Smith, L. T. 1999. *Decolonizing Methodologies: Research and Indigenous People.* London: Zed Books.

Sobande, F., and Basu, M. 2023. "Beyond BAME, WOC, and 'Political Blackness': Diasporic Digital Communing Practices." *Communication, Culture and Critique* 16:91–98.

Spivak, G. C. 1988. "Can the Subaltern Speak?" In *Marxism and the Interpretation of Culture*, edited by C. Nelson and L. Grossberg, 271–313. Basingstoke, U.K.: Macmillan Education.

———. 1991. "Neocolonialism and the Secret Agent of Knowledge." Interview with R. Young. *Oxford Literary Review*, no. 13, 220–251.

Sport England. 2021. "Active Lives Online." Accessed December 9, 2021. https://activelives.sportengland.org/.

Spracklen, K. 2008. "The Holy Blood and the Holy Grail: Myth of Scientific Racism and the Pursuit of Excellence in Sport." *Leisure Studies* 27 (2): 221–227.

Stanley, P. 2020. "Unlikely Hikers: Activism, *Instagram*, and the Queer Mobilities of Fat Hikers, Women Hiking Alone, and Hikers of Color." *Mobilities* 15 (2): 241–256.

St. Louis, B. 2003. "Sport, Genetics and the 'Natural Athlete': The Resurgence of Racial Science." *Body & Society* 9 (2): 75–95.

Sugden, J. 2010. "Critical Left Realism and Sport Interventions in Divided Societies." *International Review for the Sociology of Sport* 45 (3): 258–272.

Sundari, A., and Pearson, R. 2018. *Striking Women: Struggles and Strategies of South Asian Women Workers from Grunswick to Gate Gourmet*. London: Lawrence and Wishart.

Szto, C. 2020. *Changing on the Fly: Hockey through the Voices of South Asian Canadians*. New Brunswick, N.J.: Rutgers University Press.

Takhar, A., Maclaran, P., and Stevens, L. 2012. "Bollywood Cinema's Global Reach: Consuming the 'Diasporic Consciousness.'" *Journal of Macromarketing* 32 (3): 266–279.

Thangaraj, S. I. 2012. "Playing through Differences: Black-White Racial Logic and Interrogating South Asian American Identity." *Ethnic and Racial Studies* 35 (6): 988–1006.

———. 2015. *Desi Hoop Dreams: Pickup Basketball and the Making of Asian American Masculinity*. New York: New York University Press.

———. 2017. "'Say Her Name!' Confronting Erasure, Rethinking Possibilities for a Democratic Future." Tropics of Meta, July 13, 2017. https://tropicsofmeta.com/2017/07/13/say-her-name-confronting-erasure-rethinking-possibilities-for-a-democratic-future/.

———. 2022. "Masculinities." *Feminist Anthropology* 3:254–262.

Thangaraj, S. I., Arnaldo, C. R., Jr., and Chin, C. B. 2016. *Asian American Sporting Cultures*. New York: New York University Press.

Thangaraj, S., Ratna, A., Burdsey, D., and Rand, E. 2018. "Leisure and the Racing of National Populism." *Leisure Studies* 37 (6): 648–661.

Tillmann, L. N. 2015. *In Solidarity: Friendship, Family, and Activism beyond Gay and Straight*. New York: Routledge.

Tolia-Kelly, D. 2004a. "Landscape, Race and Memory: Biographical Mapping of the Routes of British Asian Landscape Values." *Landscape Research* 29 (3): 277–292.

———. 2004b. "Materializing Post-colonial Geographies: Examining the Textural Landscapes of Migration in the South Asian Home." *Geoforum* 35 (6): 675–688.

Tredway, K. 2019. "Serena Williams and (the Perception of) Violence: Intersectionality, Performance of Blackness, and Women's Professional Tennis." *Ethnic and Racial Studies* 43 (9): 1563–1580.

Trussell, D. E., and Jeanes, R., eds. 2021. *Families, Sport, Leisure and Social Justice: From Protest to Progress.* Oxford: Routledge.

Tuck, E., and Yang, K. W. 2012. "Decolonization Is Not a Metaphor." *Decolonization: Indigeneity, Education & Society* 1 (1): 1–40.

———. 2014. "Unbecoming Claims: Pedagogies of Refusal in Qualitative Research." *Qualitative Inquiry* 20 (6): 811–818.

van Ingen, C. 2013. "'Seeing What Frames Our Seeing': Seeking Histories on Early Black Female Boxers." *Journal of Sport History* 40 (1): 93–110.

Vergès, F. 2021. *A Decolonial Feminism.* London: Pluto Press.

Vincent, C., Neal, S., and Iqbal, H. 2018. *Friendship and Diversity: Class, Ethnicity and Social Relationships in the City.* Cham, Switzerland: Palgrave Macmillan.

Virali, P., and Rao, V. 2019. "Hinduism and the Legacy of Casteism." *Bharatiya Manyaprad* 7 (1): 50–55.

Virdee, S. 2014. *Racism, Class and the Racialised Outsider.* London: Springer Nature.

Wagg, S., ed. 2004. *British Football and Social Exclusion.* London: Routledge.

Watson, B., and Scraton, S. 2001. "Confronting Whiteness? Researching the Leisure Lives of South Asian Mothers." *Journal of Gender Studies* 10 (3): 265–277.

———. 2017. "Re-confronting Whiteness: Ongoing Challenges in Sport and Leisure Research." In Ratna and Samie, *Race, Gender and Sport*, 85–106.

Webster, C. 2022. "The (In)Significance of Footballing Pleasures in the Lives of Forced Migrant Men." *Sport in Society* 25 (3): 523–536.

Whittaker, R. 2011. "The Politics of Friendship in Feminist Anthropology." *Anthropology in Action* 18 (1): 56–66.

Williamson, R. 2016. "Everyday Space, Mobile Subjects and Place-Based Belonging in Suburban Sydney." *Journal of Ethnic and Migration Studies* 42 (15): 2328–2344.

Wilson, A. 2006. *Dreams, Questions, and Struggles: South Asian Women in Britain*. London: Pluto Press.

Yep, K. S. 2012. "Peddling Sport: Liberal Multiculturalism and the Racial Triangulation of Blackness, Chineseness and Native American-ness in Professional Basketball." *Ethnic and Racial Studies* 35 (6): 971–987.

Yuval-Davis, N., Wemyss, G., and Cassidy, K. 2018. "Everyday Bordering, Belonging and the Reorientation of British Immigration Legislation." *Sociology* 52 (2): 228–244.

Index

About the Author

AARTI RATNA teaches and writes about race, gender, and popular culture, focusing on the sport and leisure engagements of British Asian girls and women. They co-edited *Gender, Race and Sport: The Politics of Ethnic "Other" Girls and Women* and are an associate professor in the Department of Social Sciences at Northumbria University in Newcastle, UK.

Available titles in the Critical Issues in Sport and Society series: